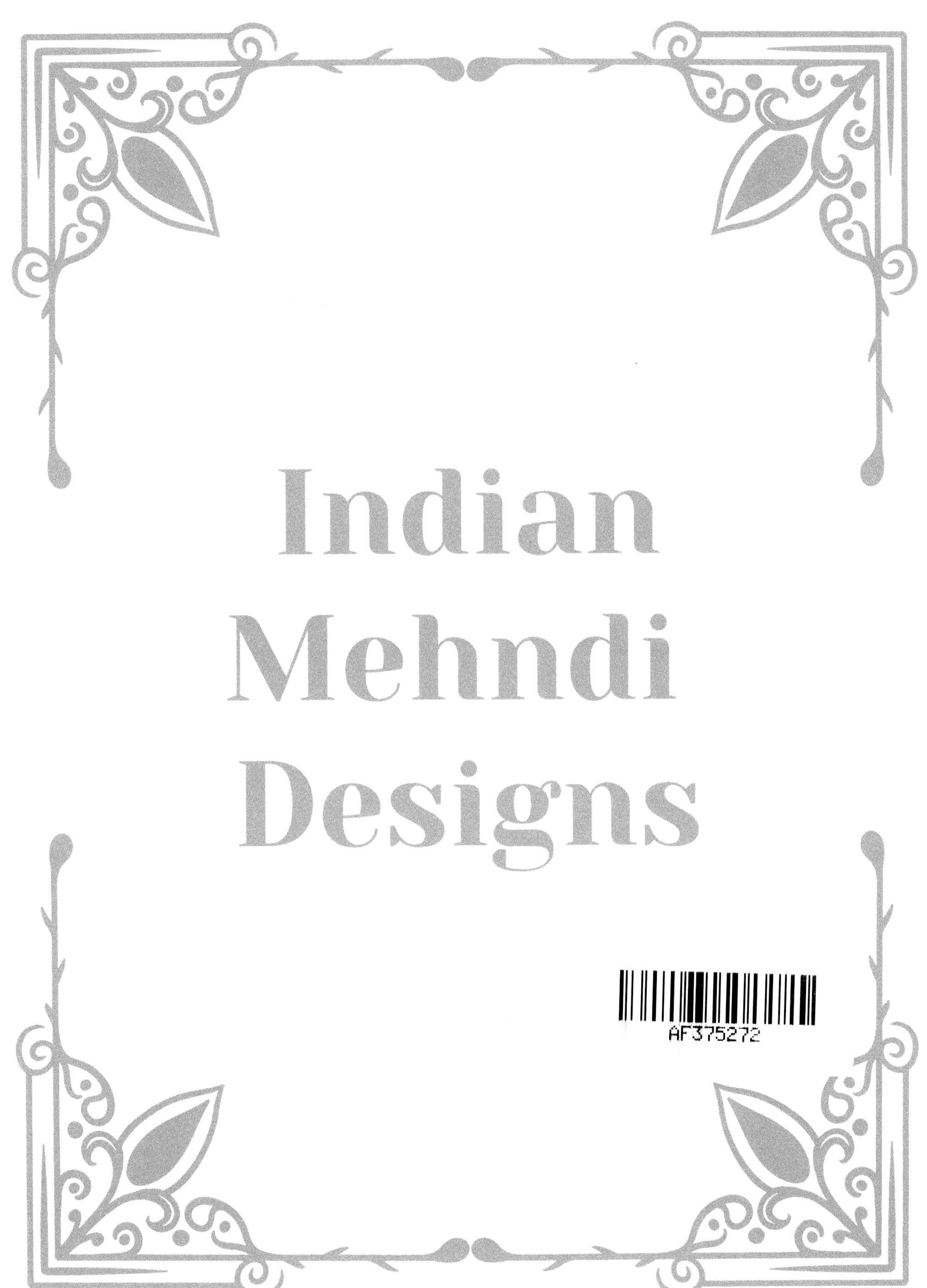

Indian Mehndi Designs

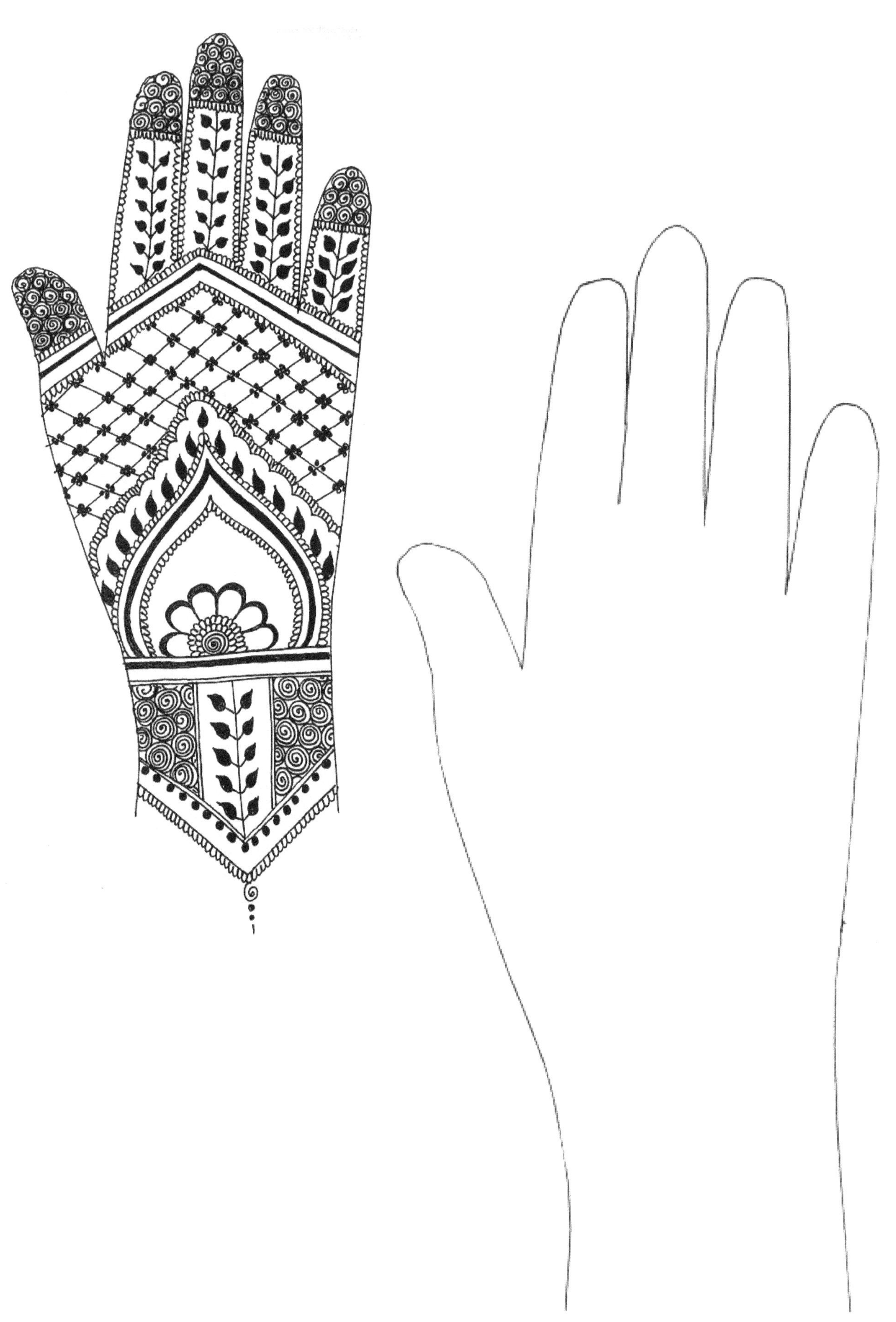

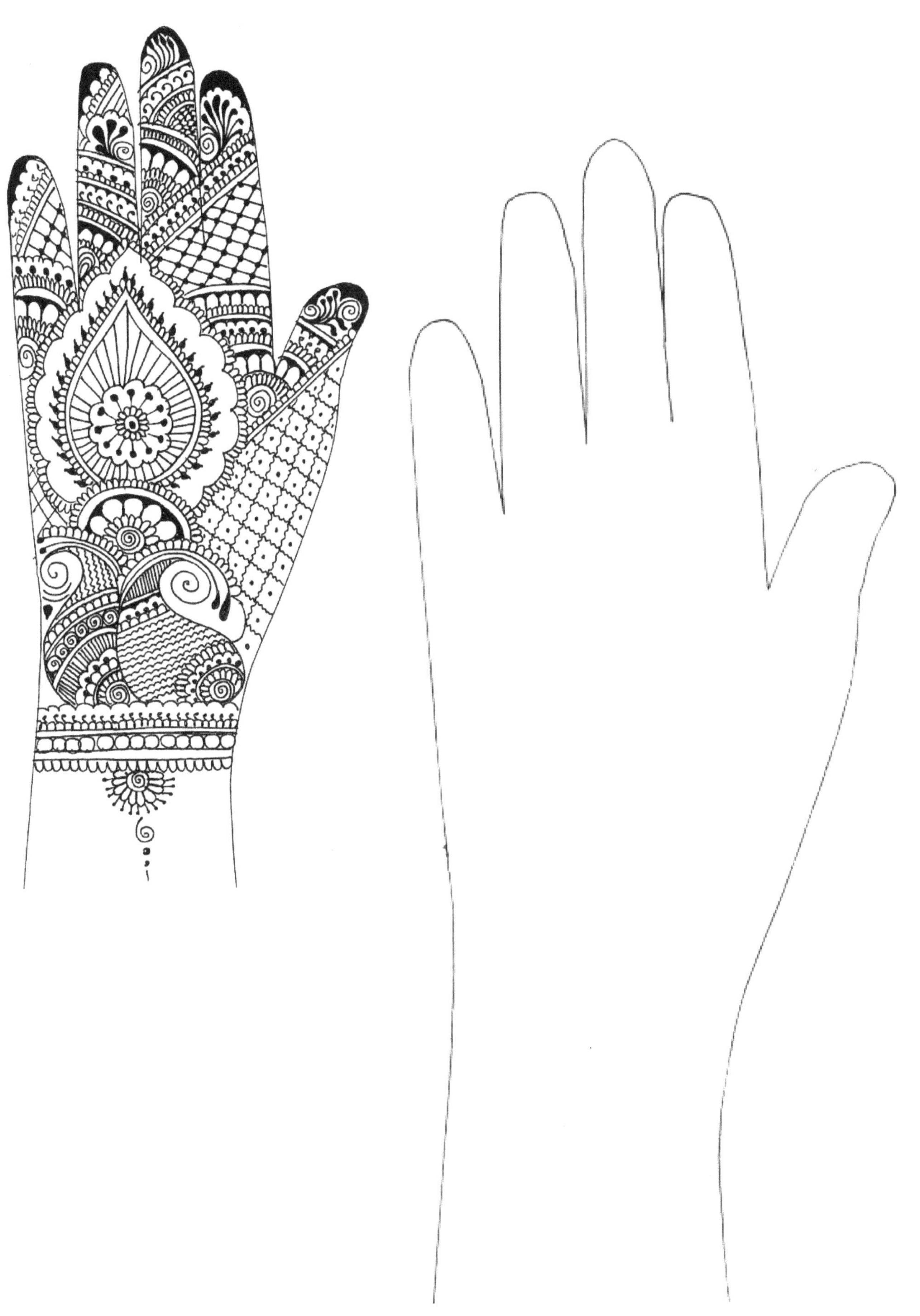

03

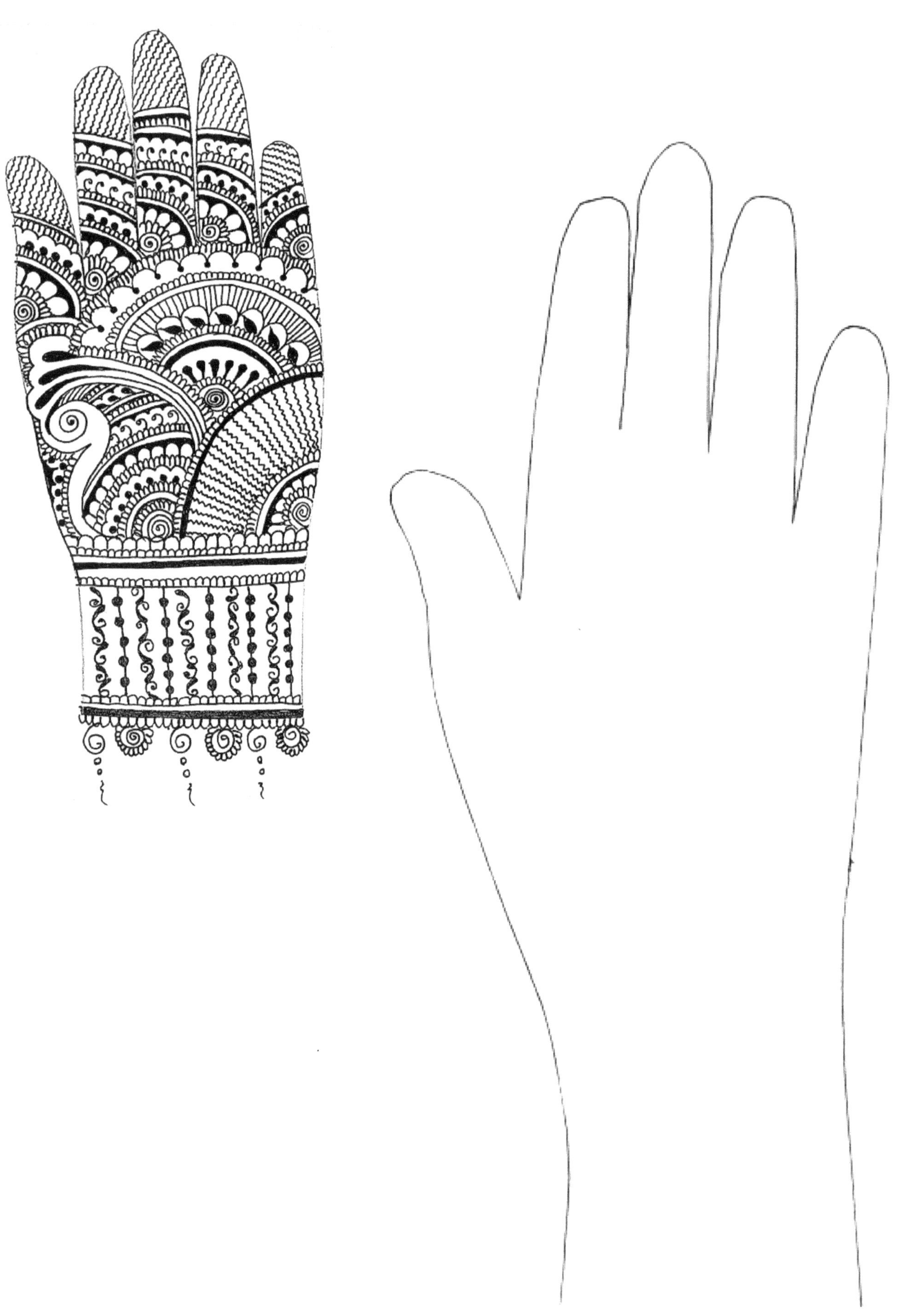

04

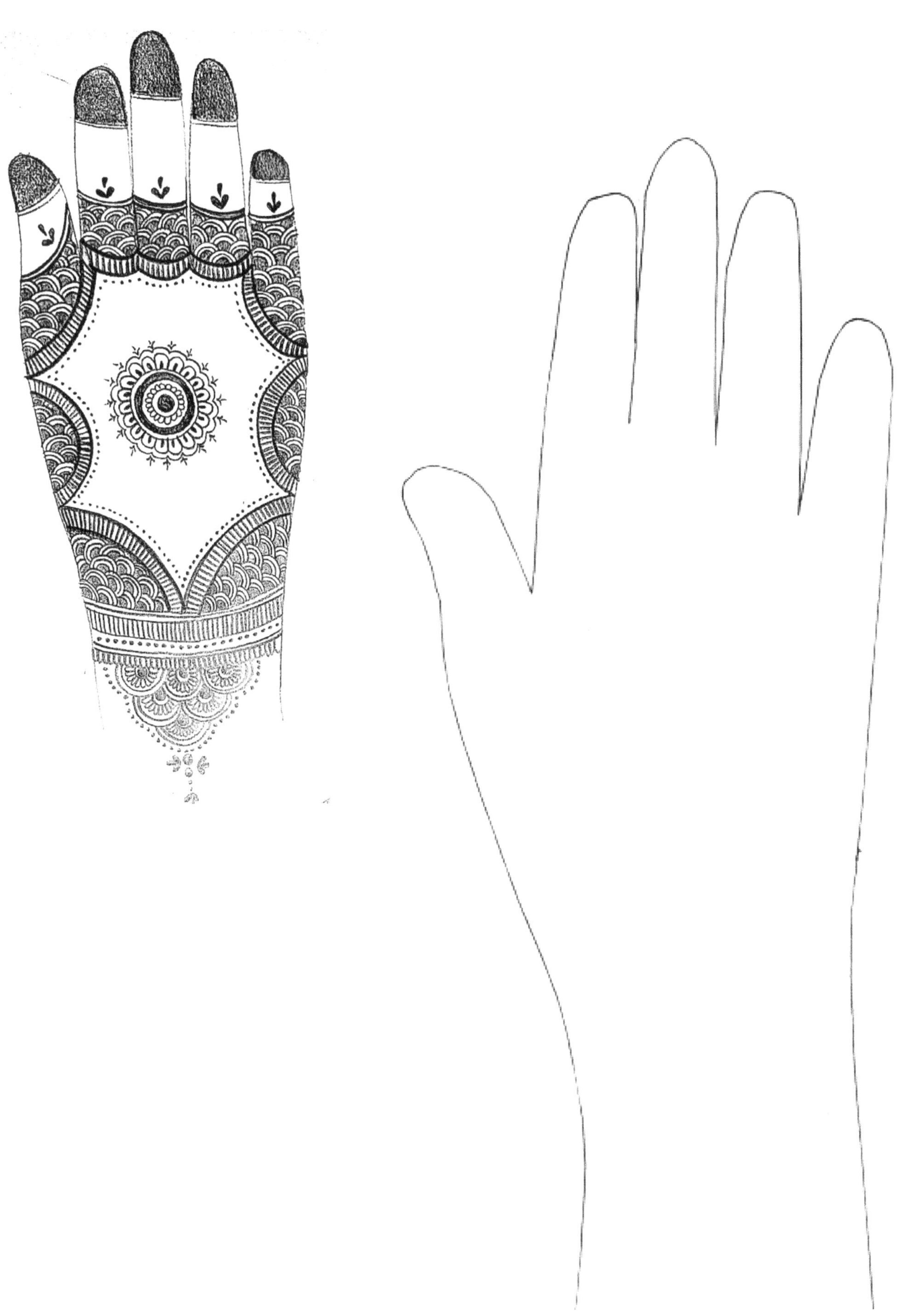

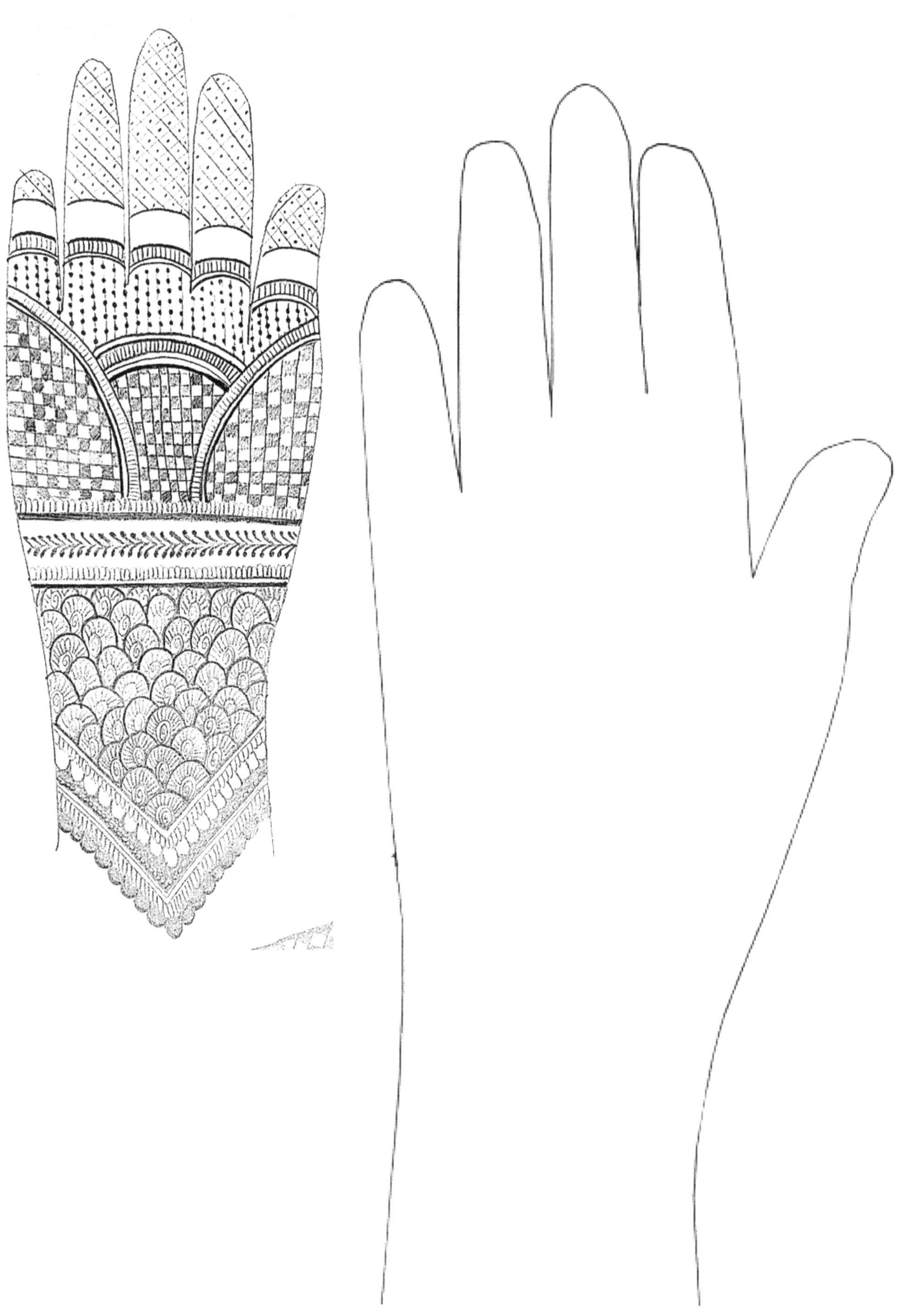

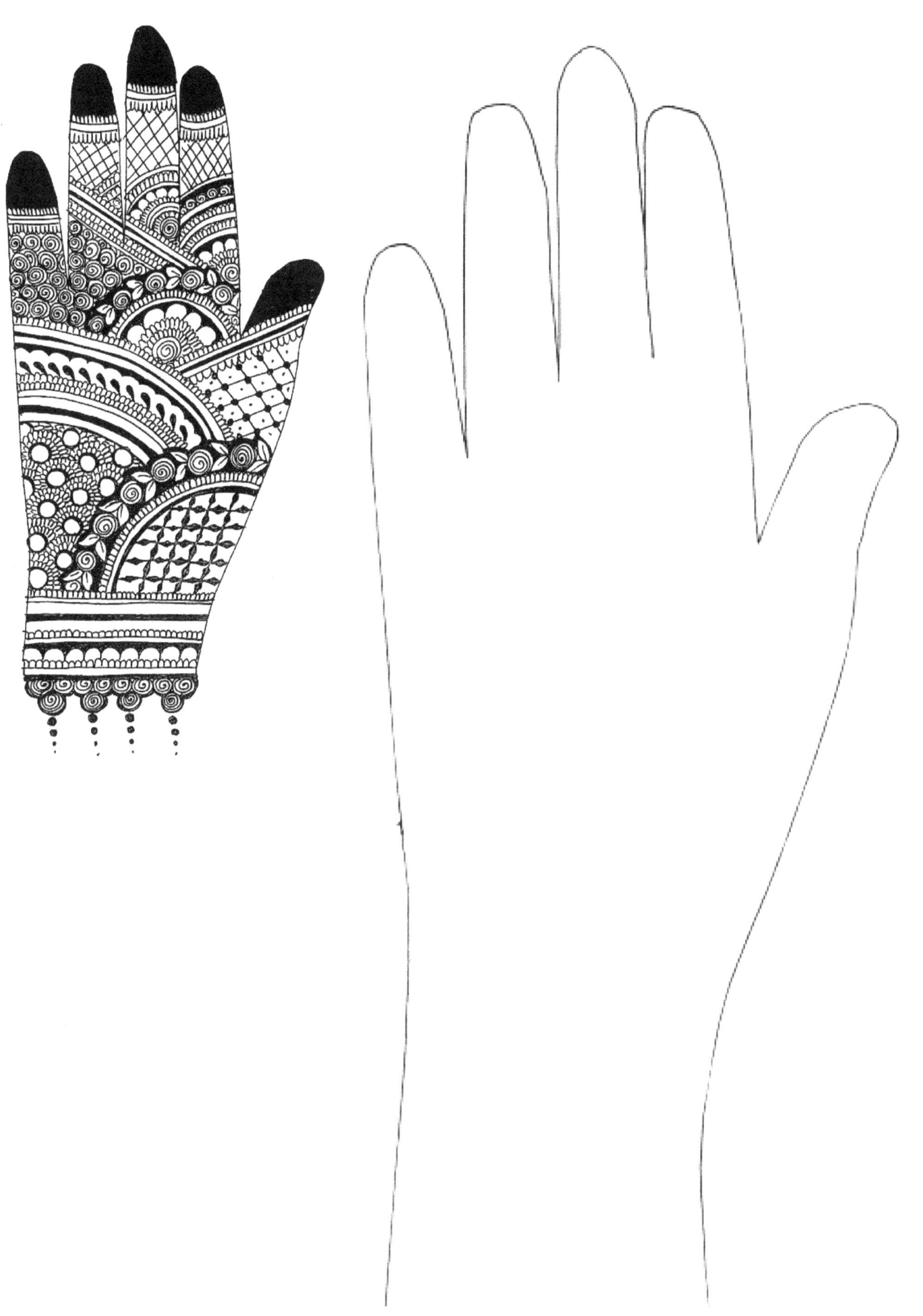

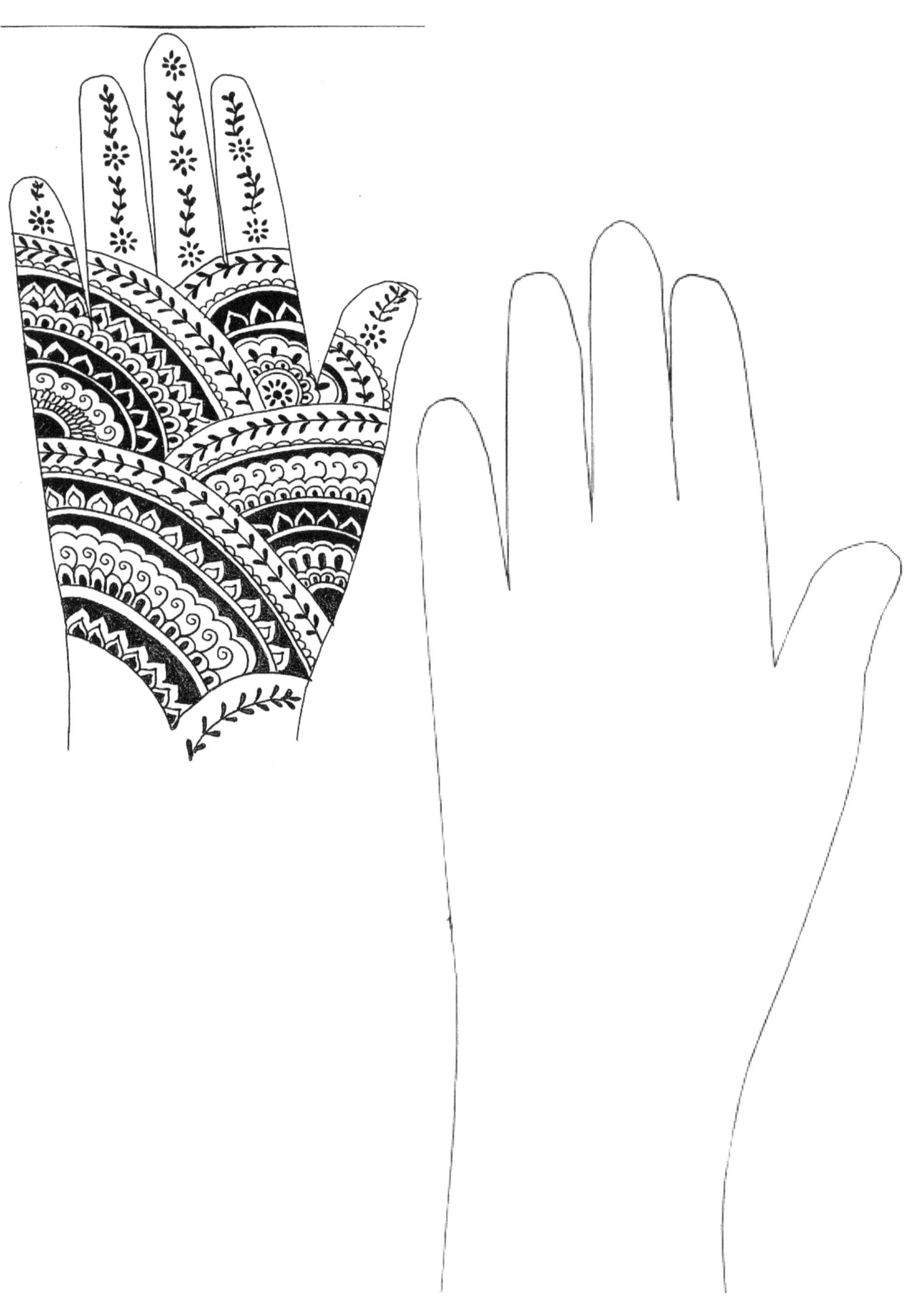

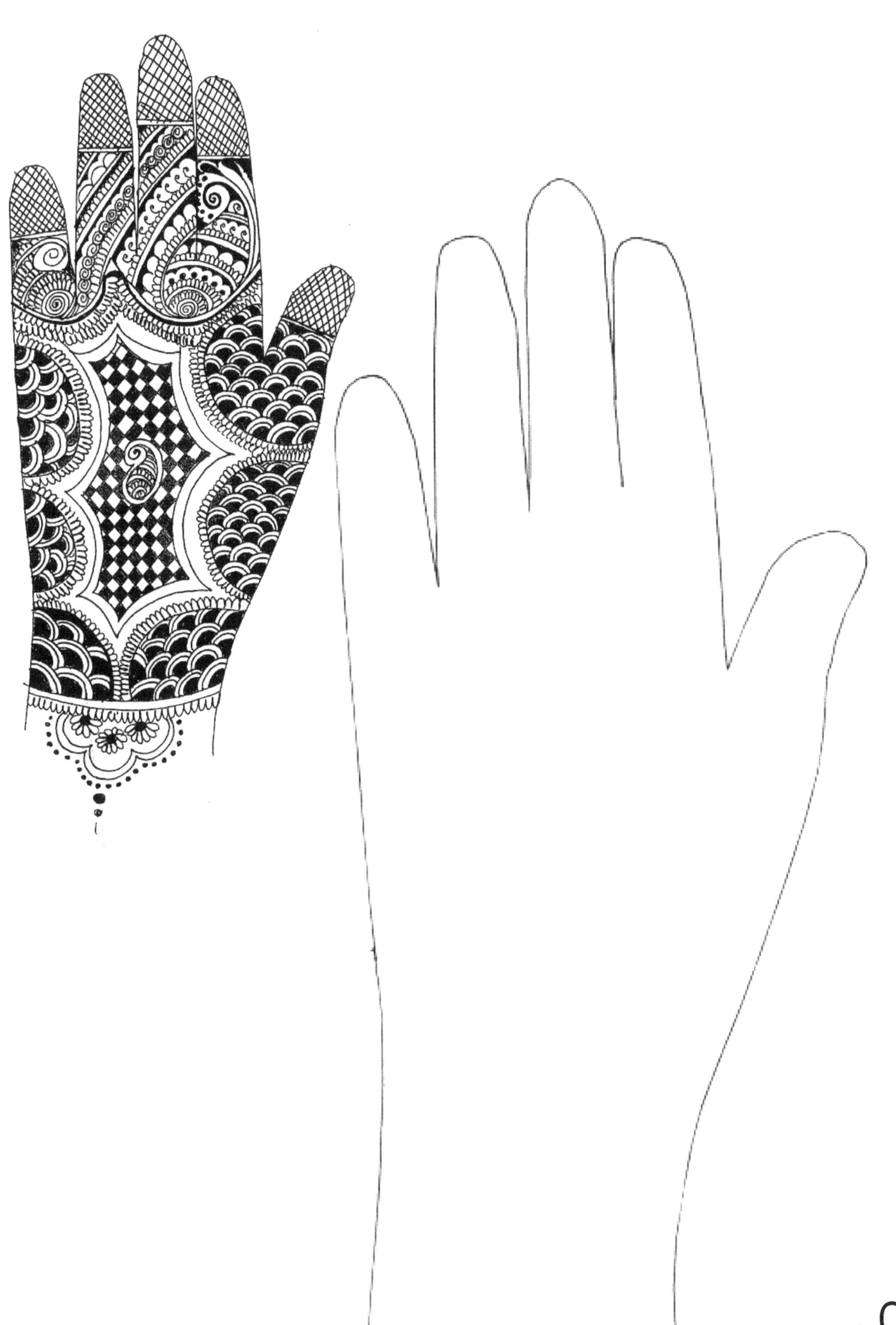

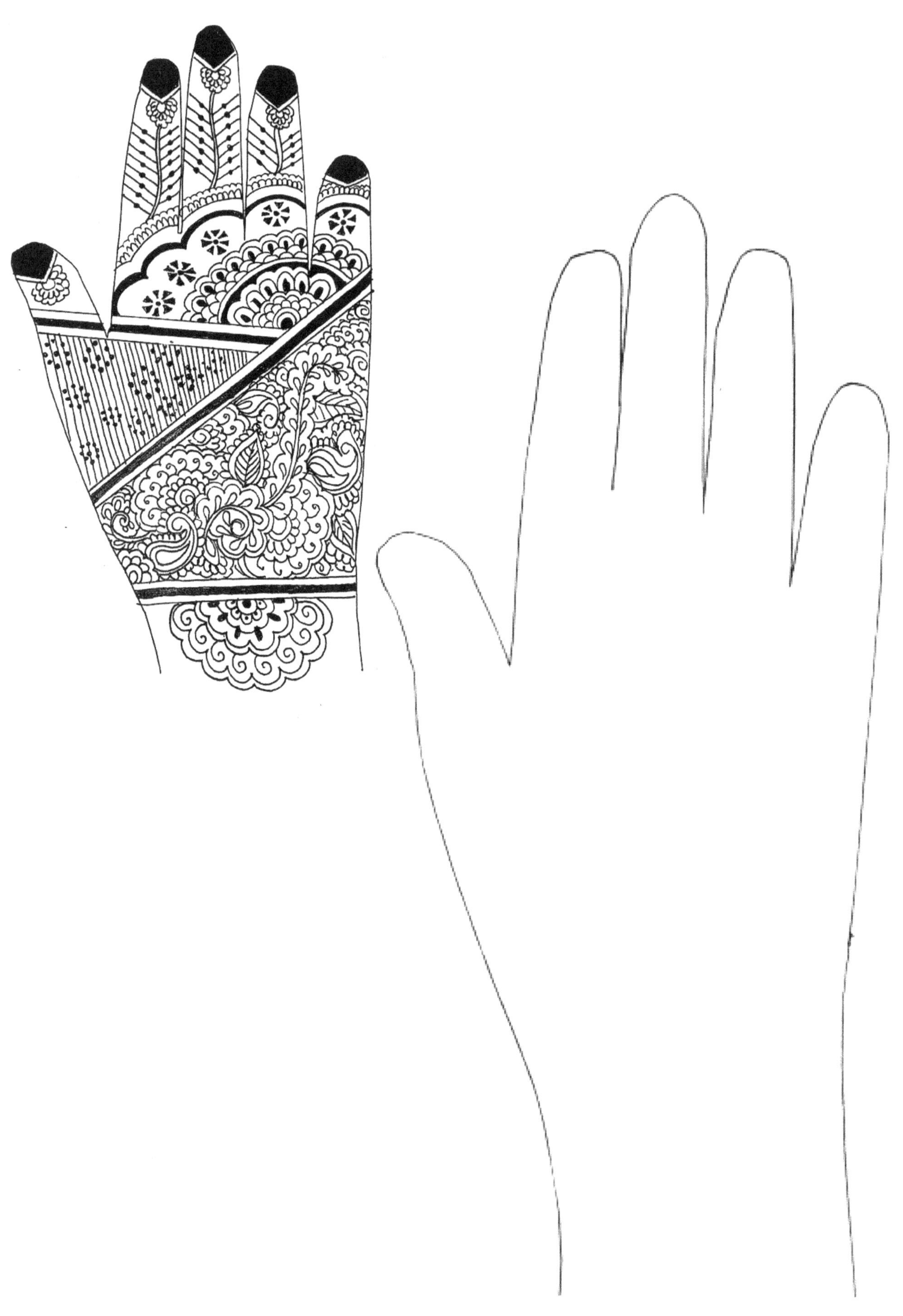

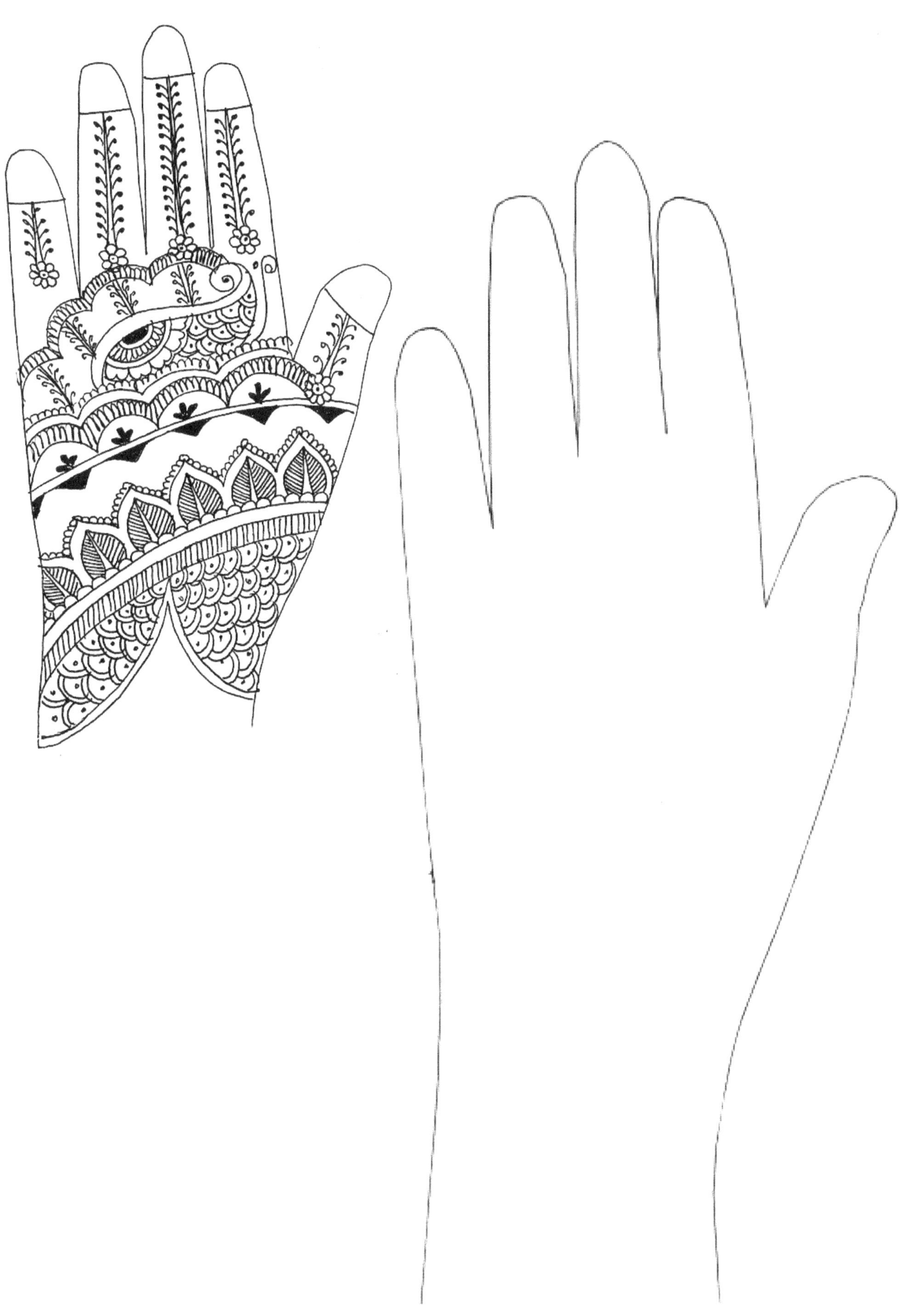

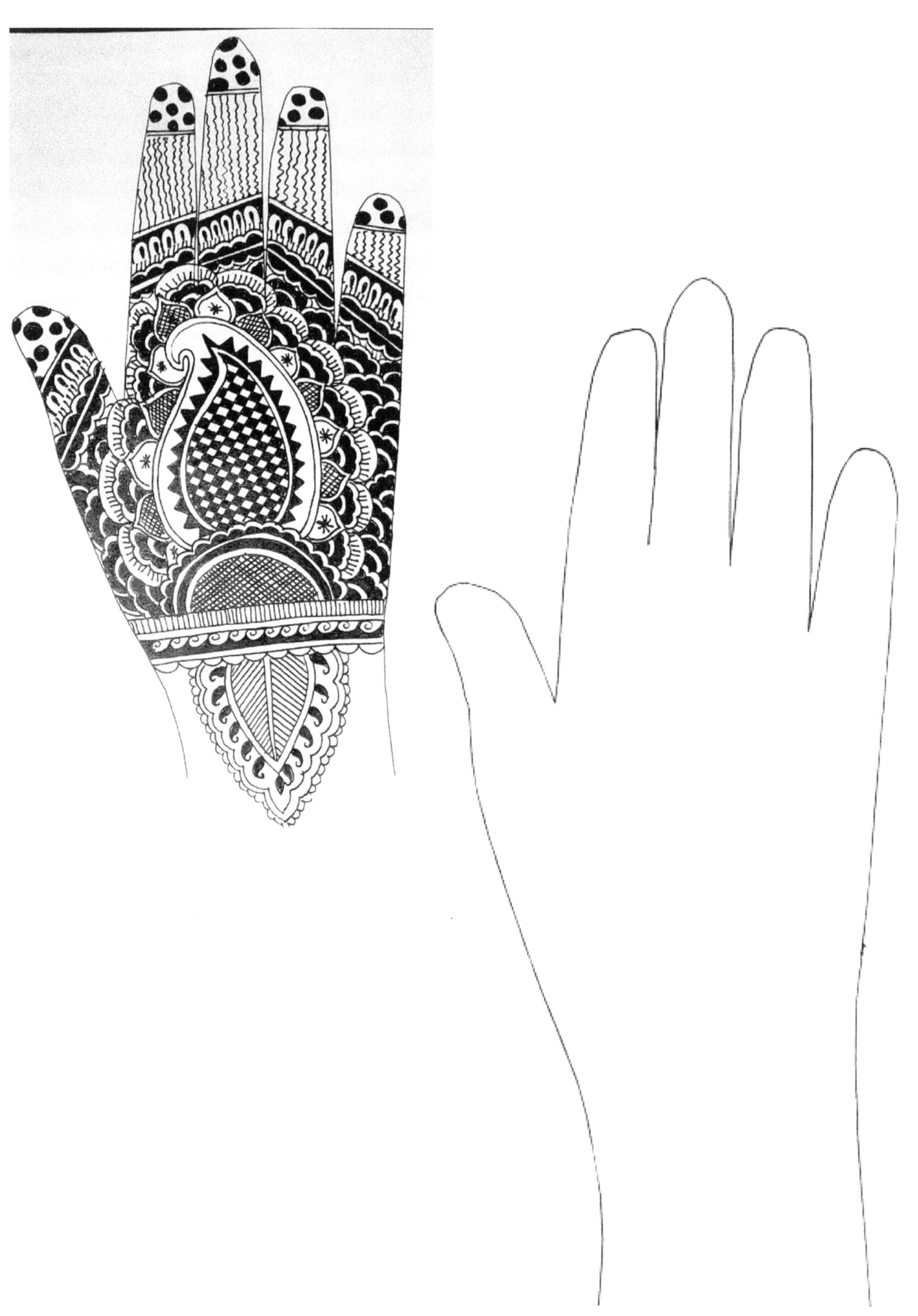

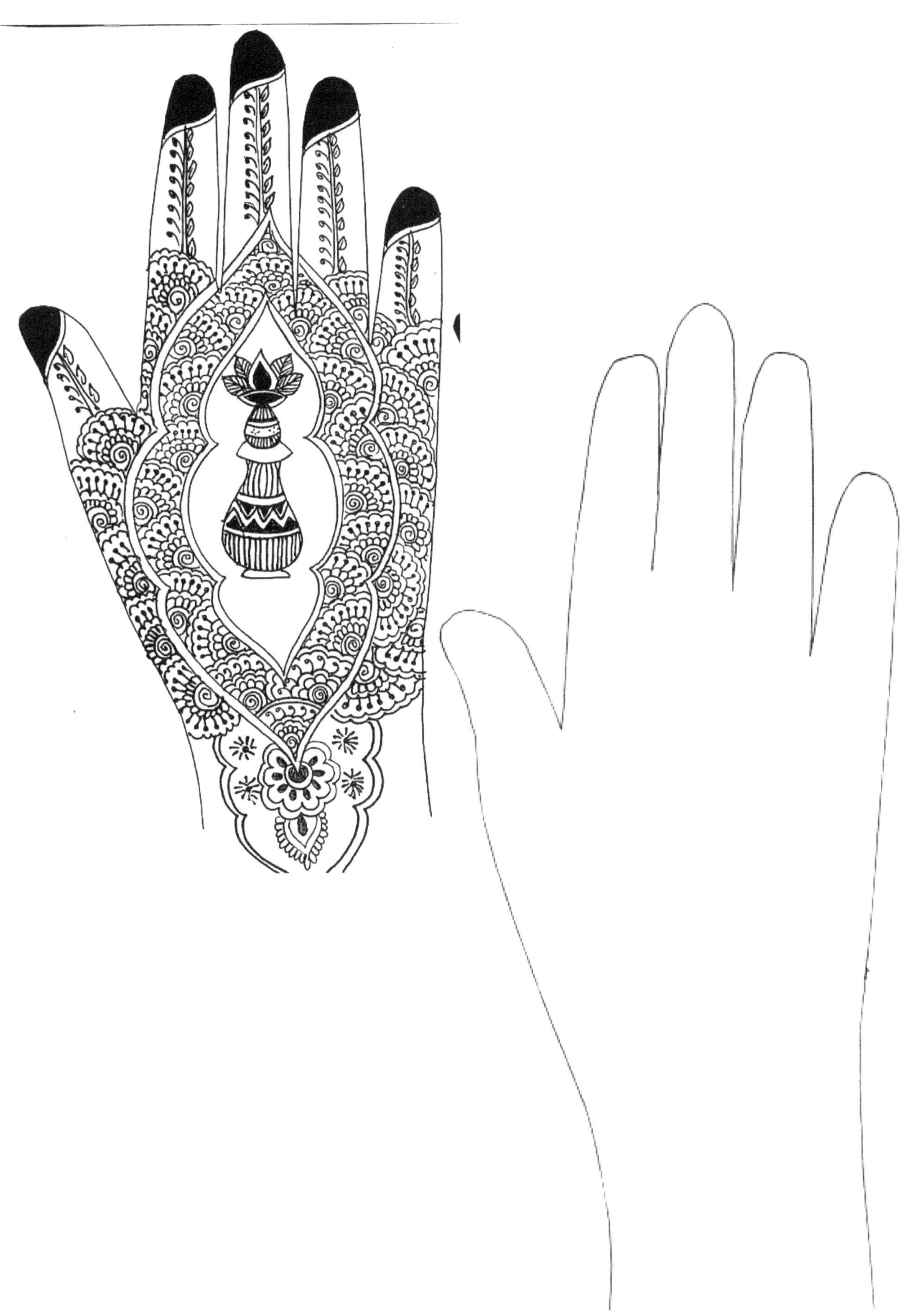

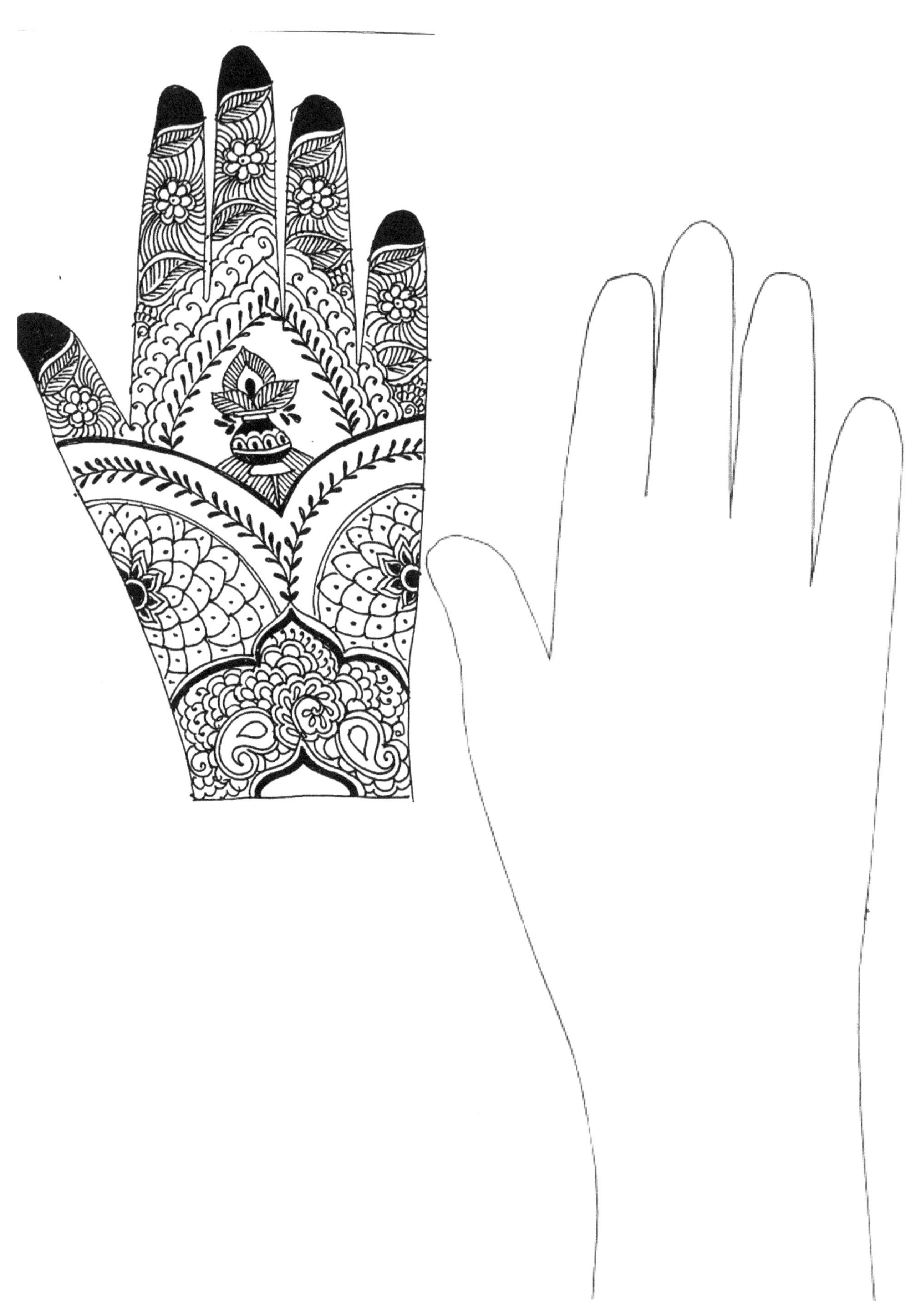

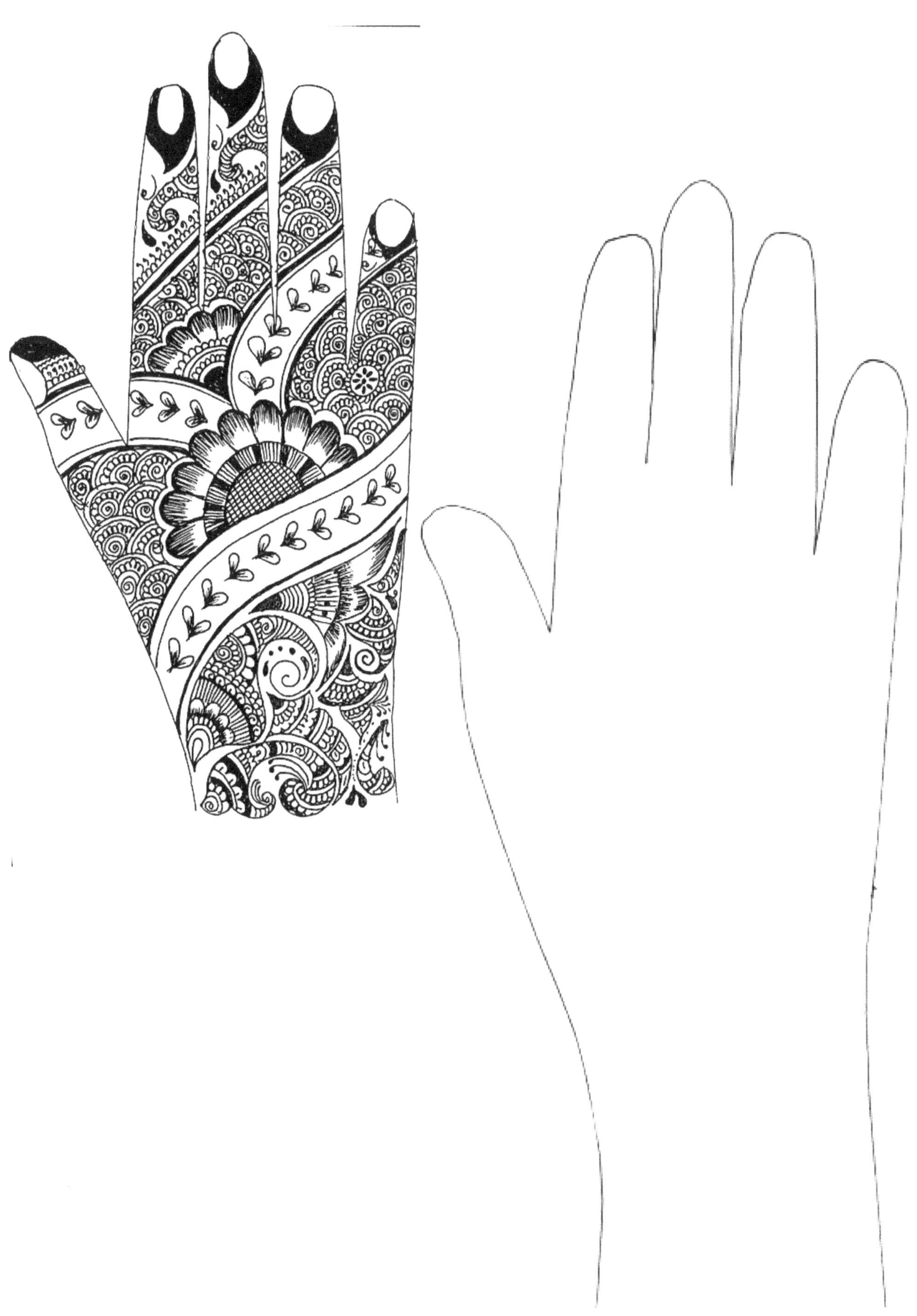

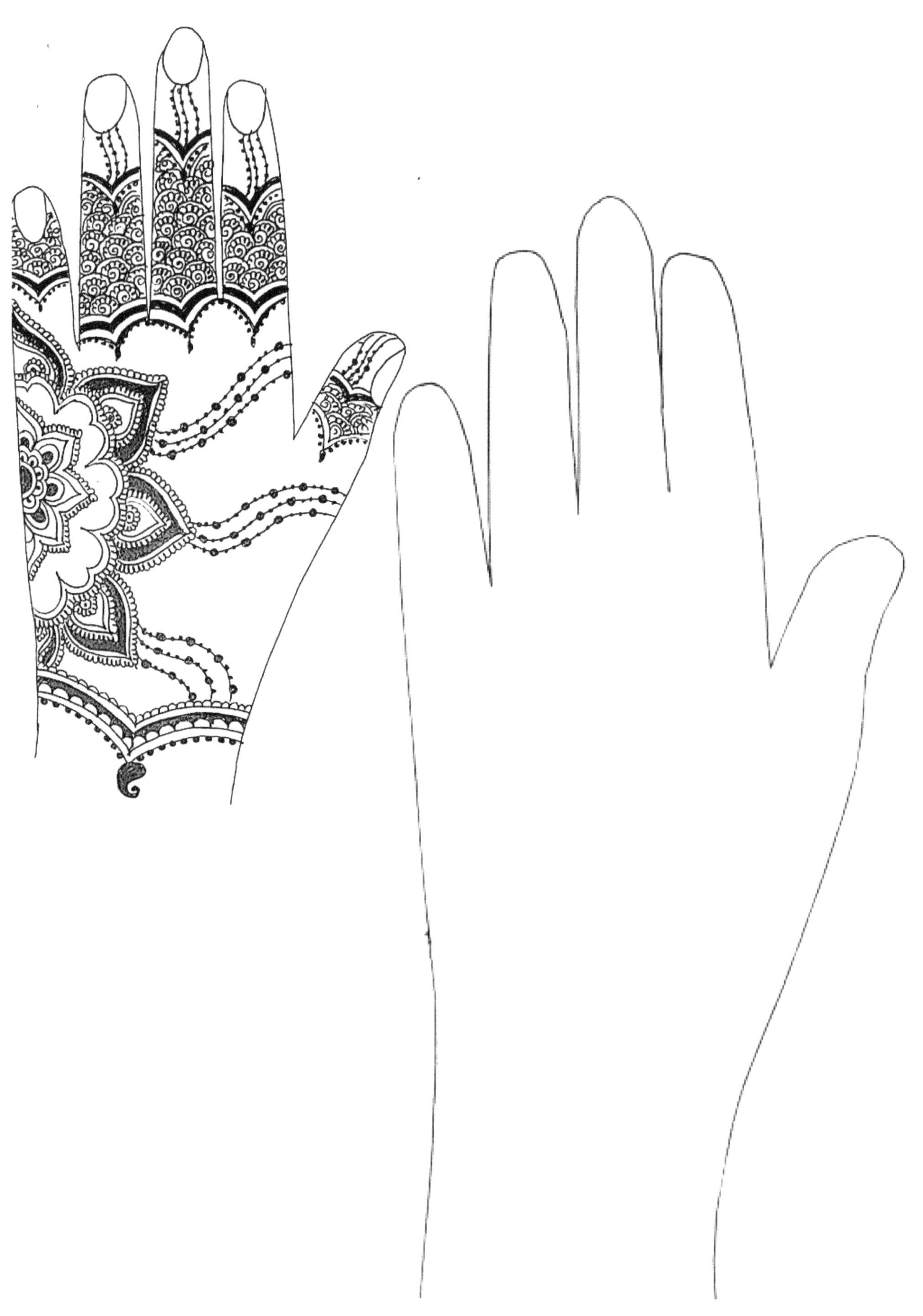

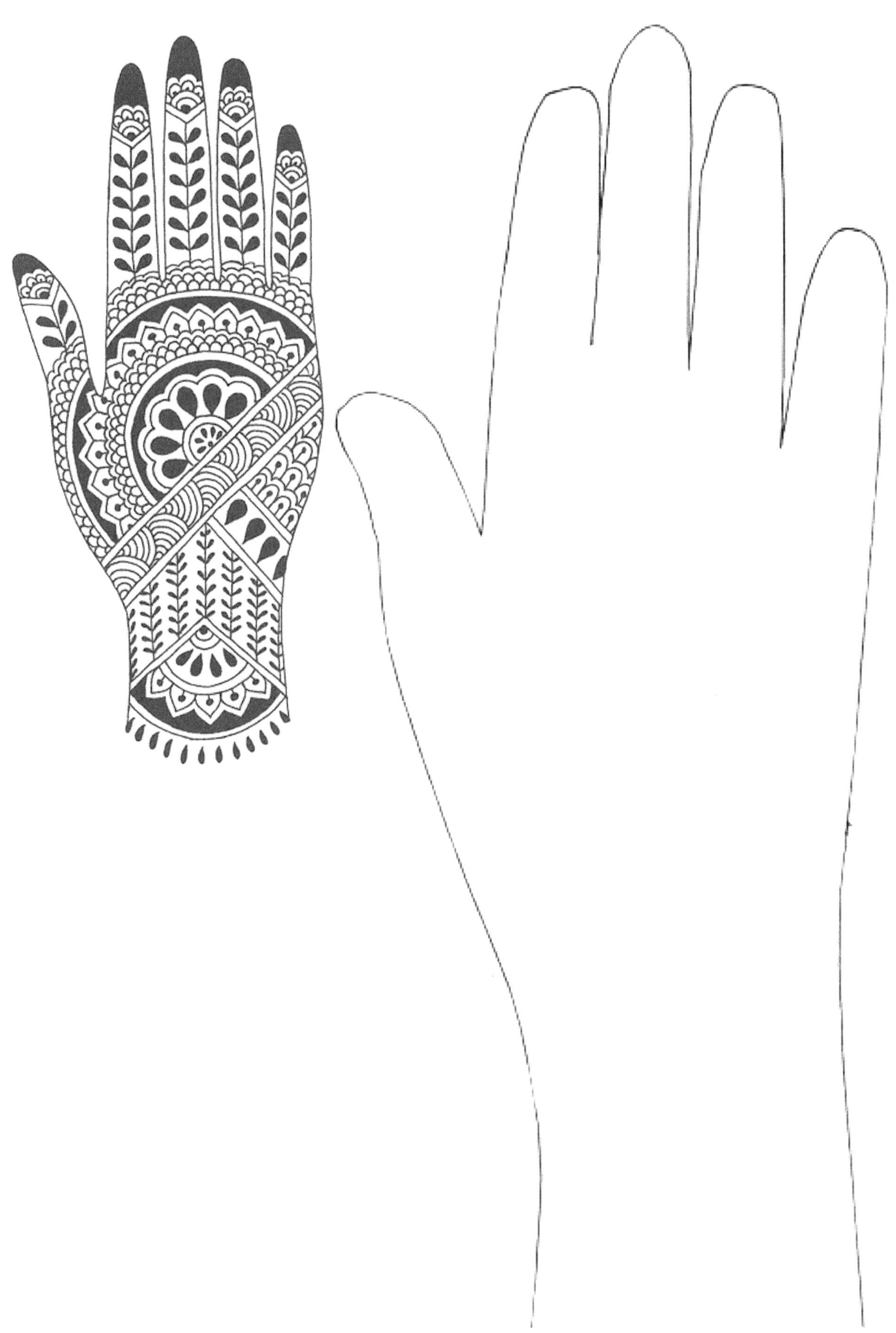

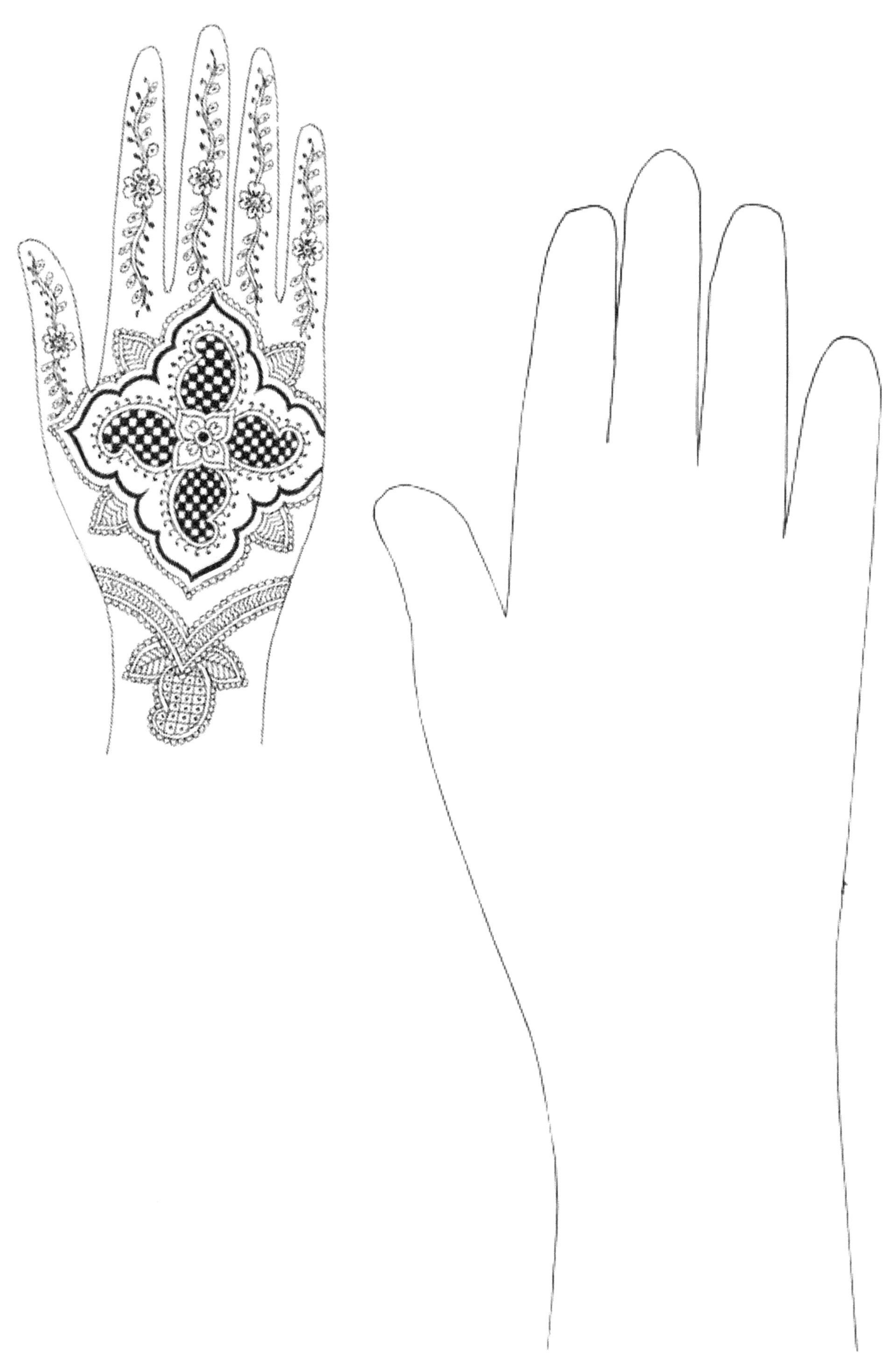

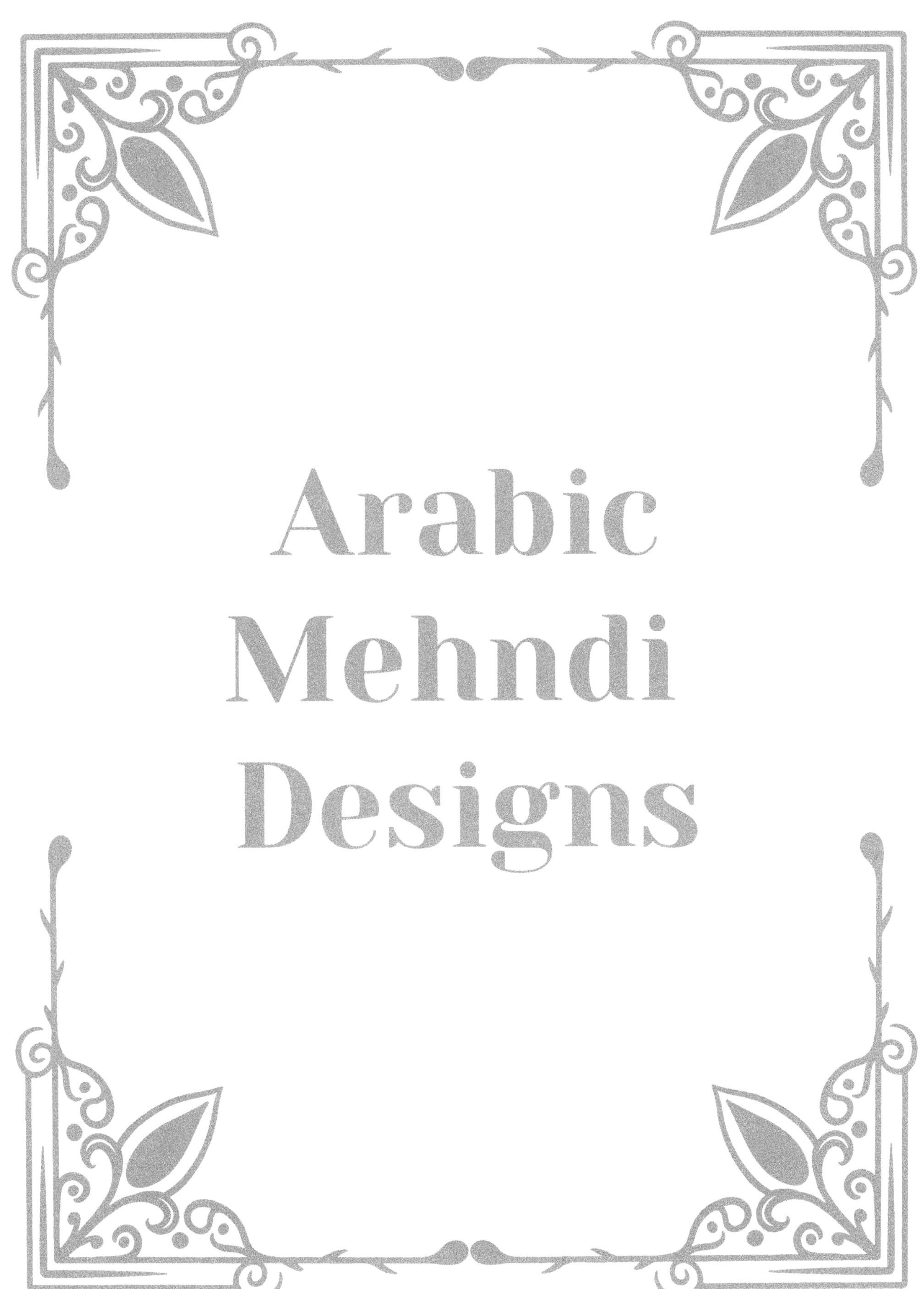

Arabic Mehndi Designs

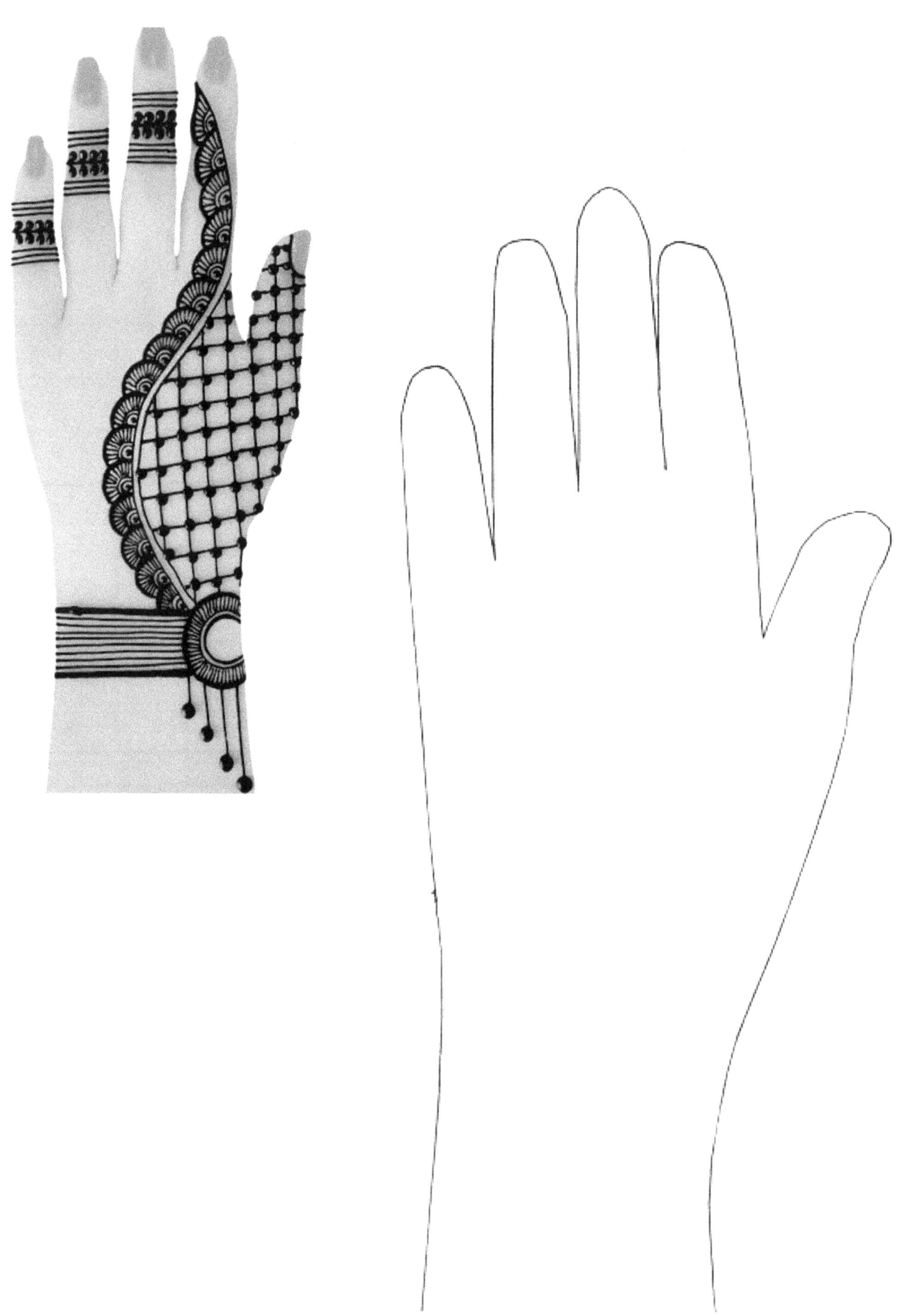

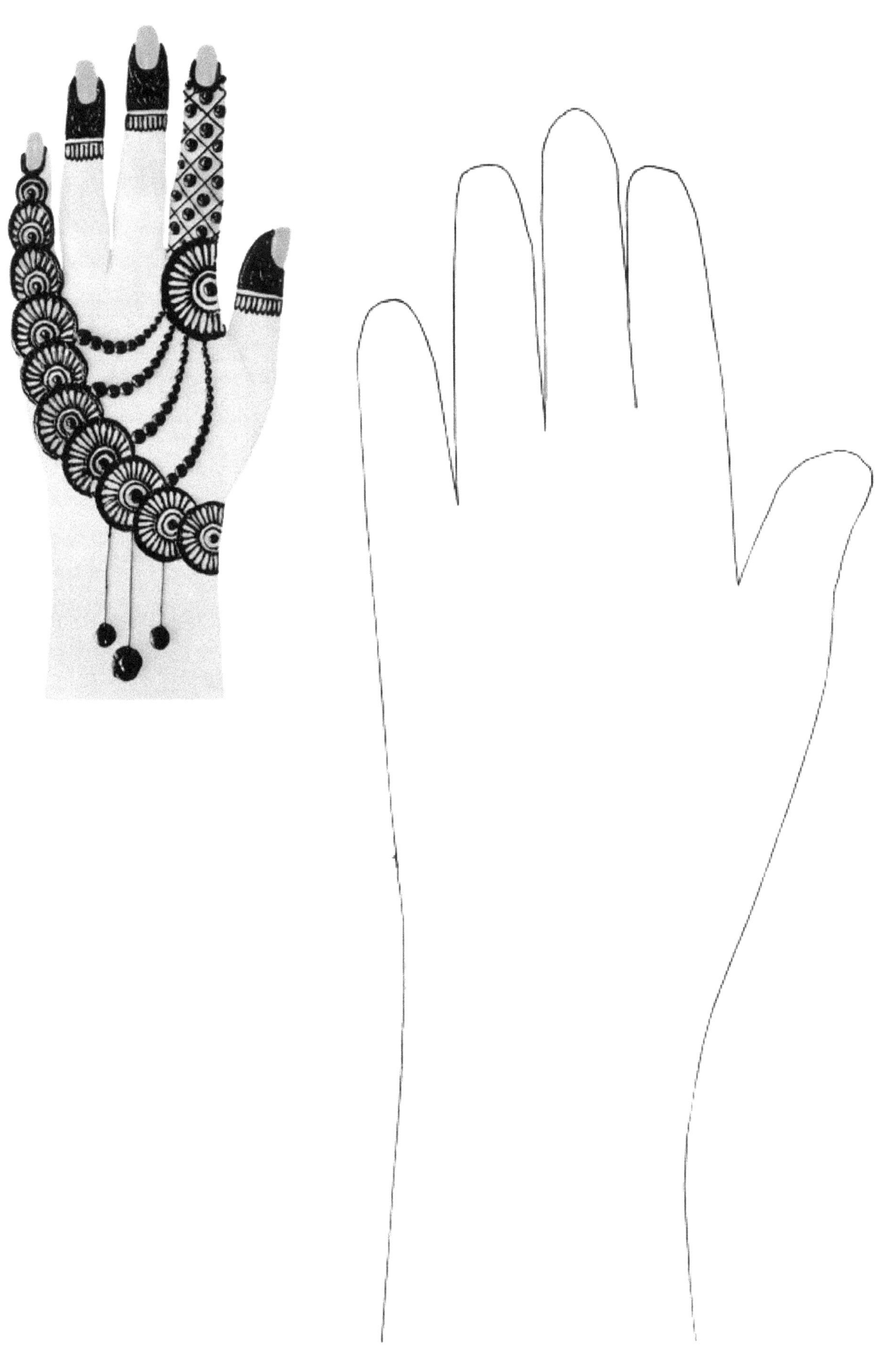

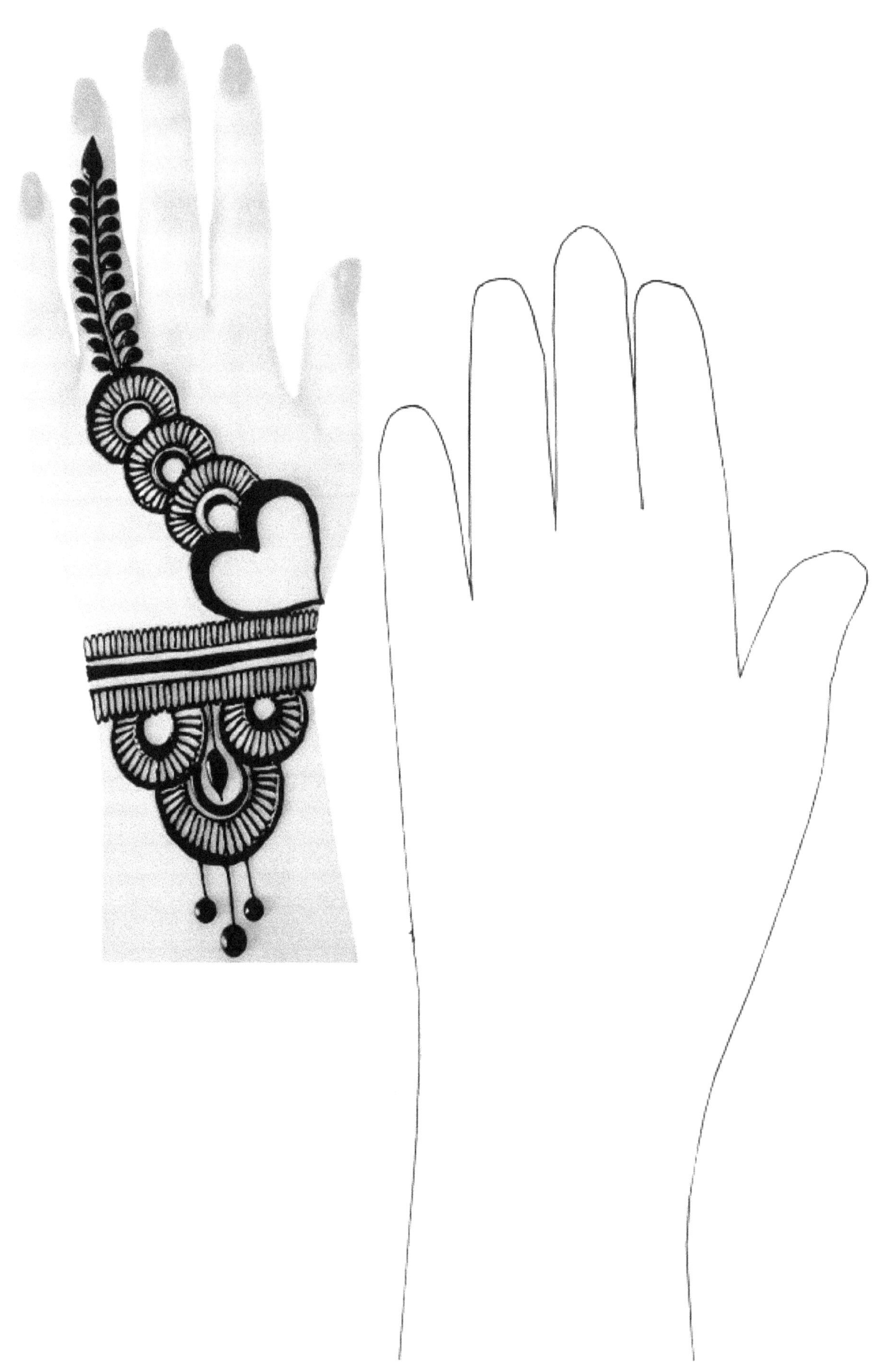

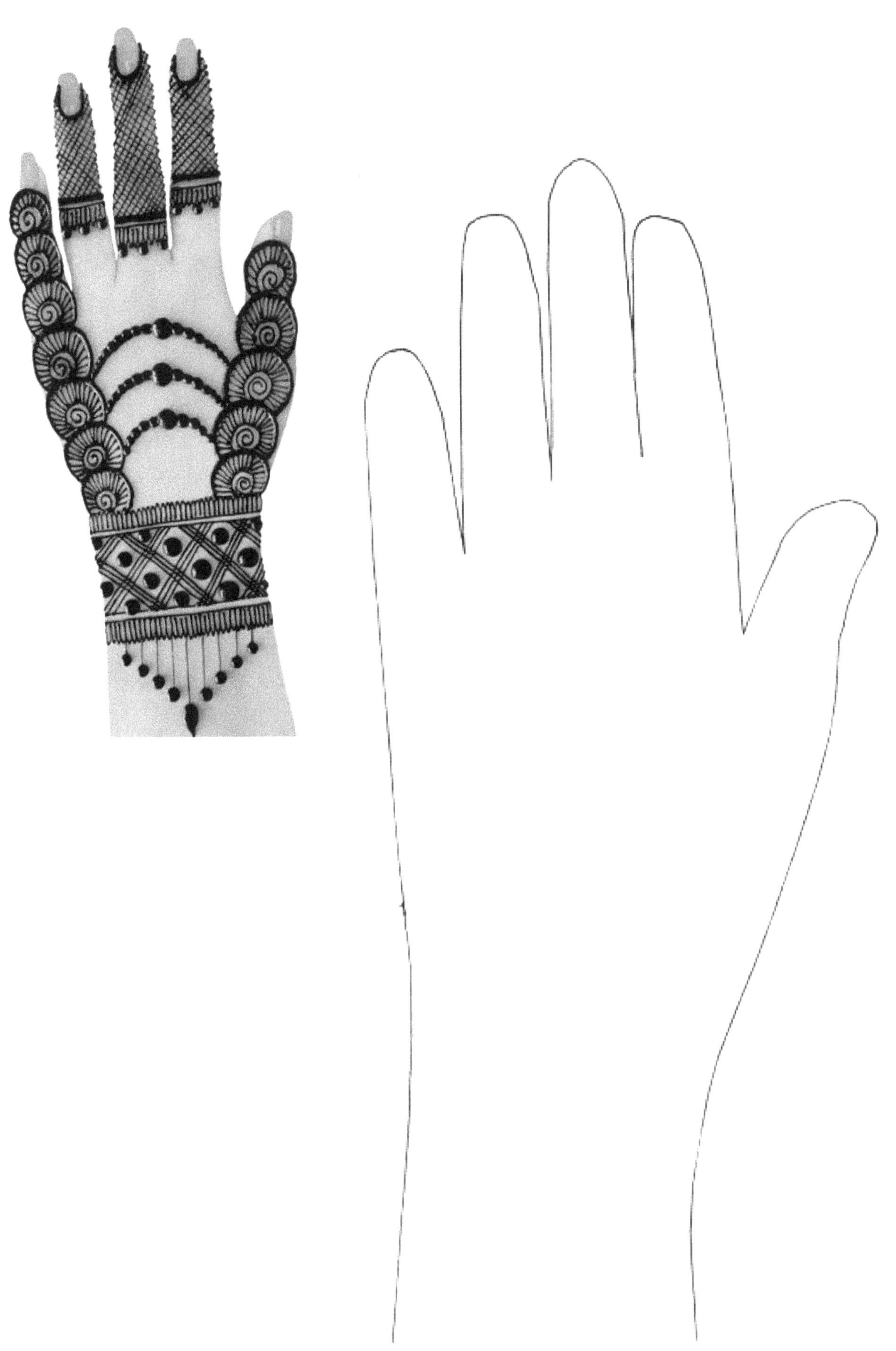

23

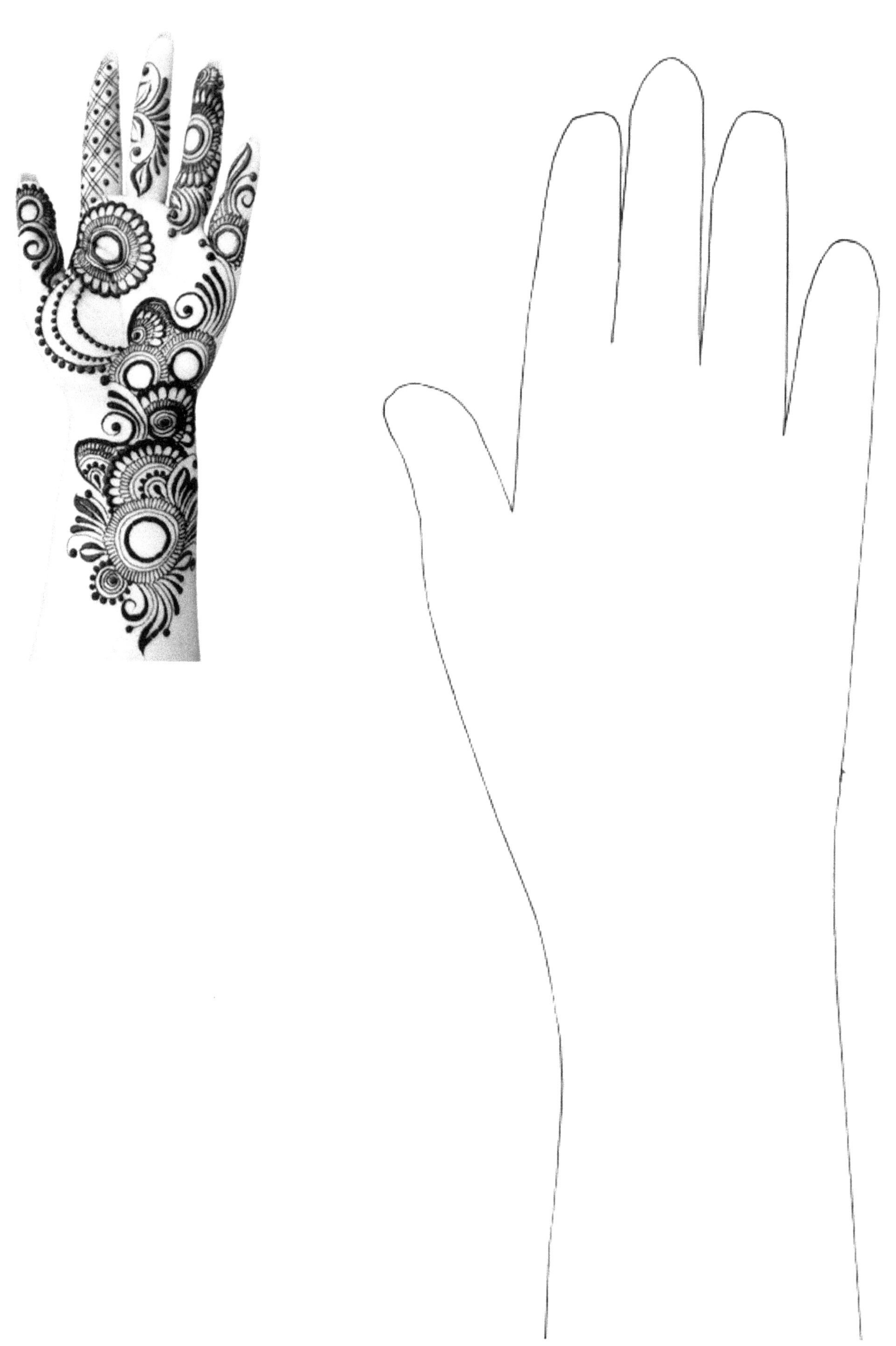

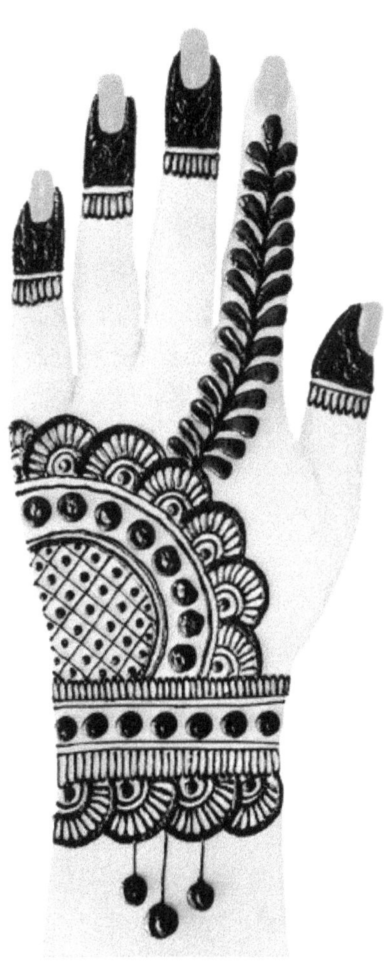

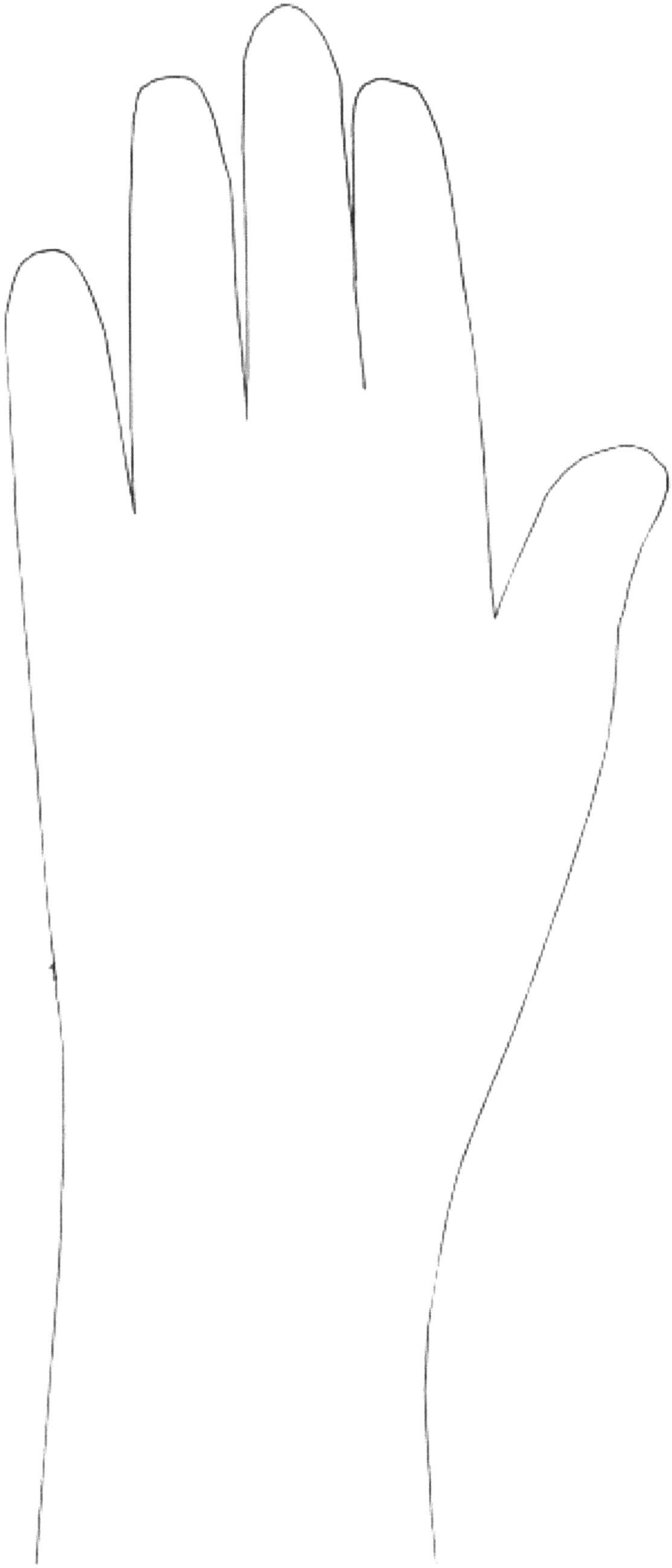

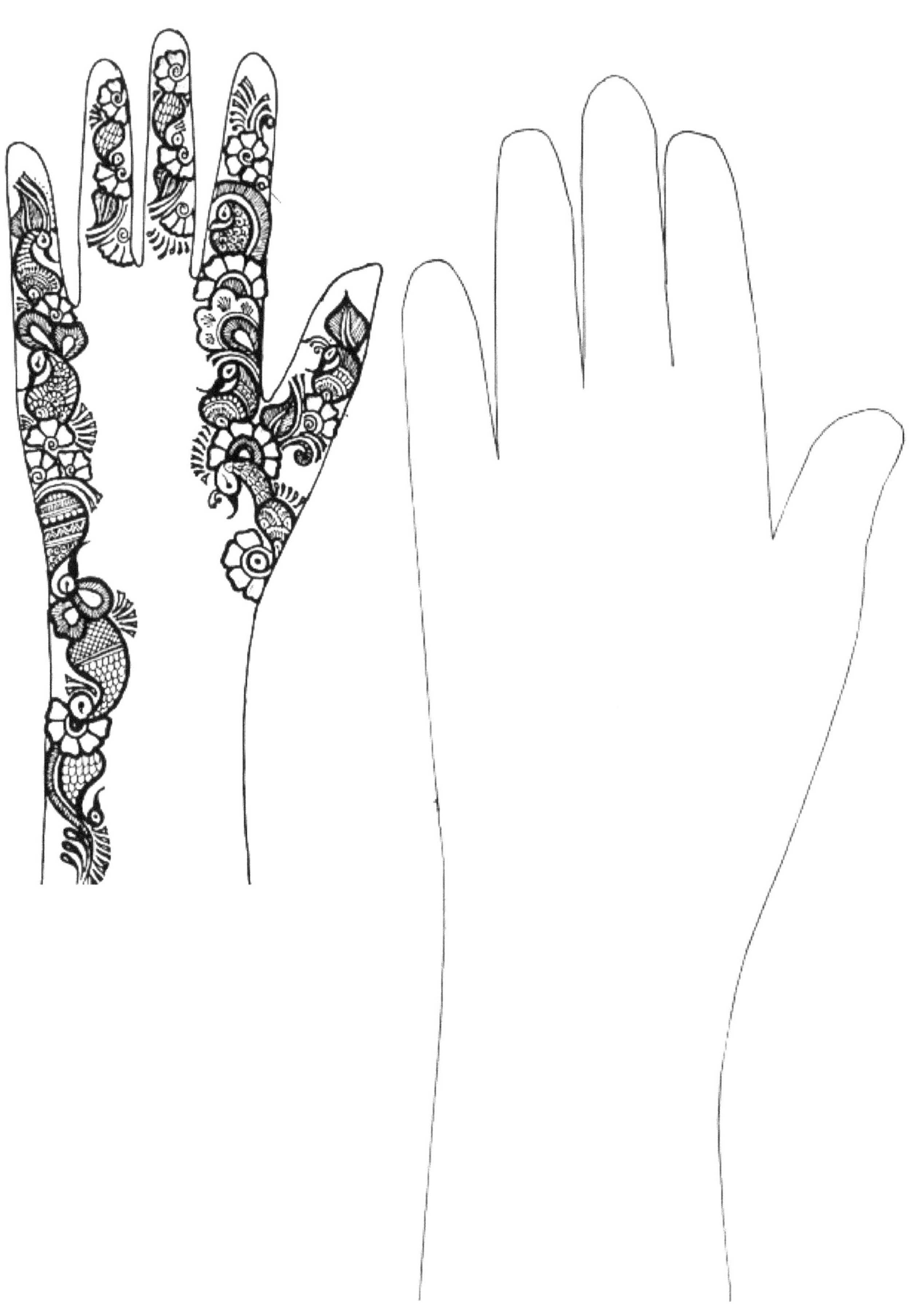

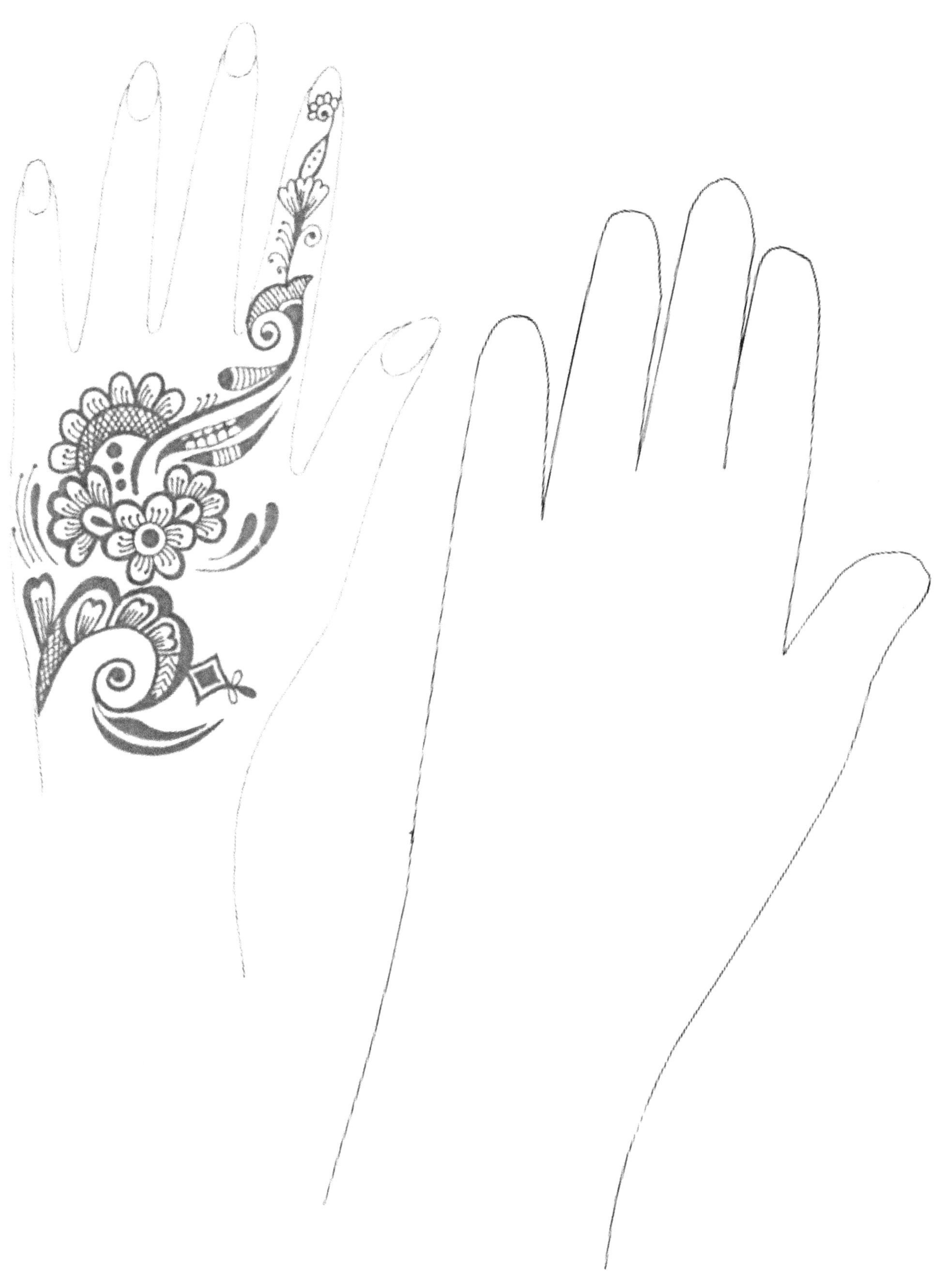

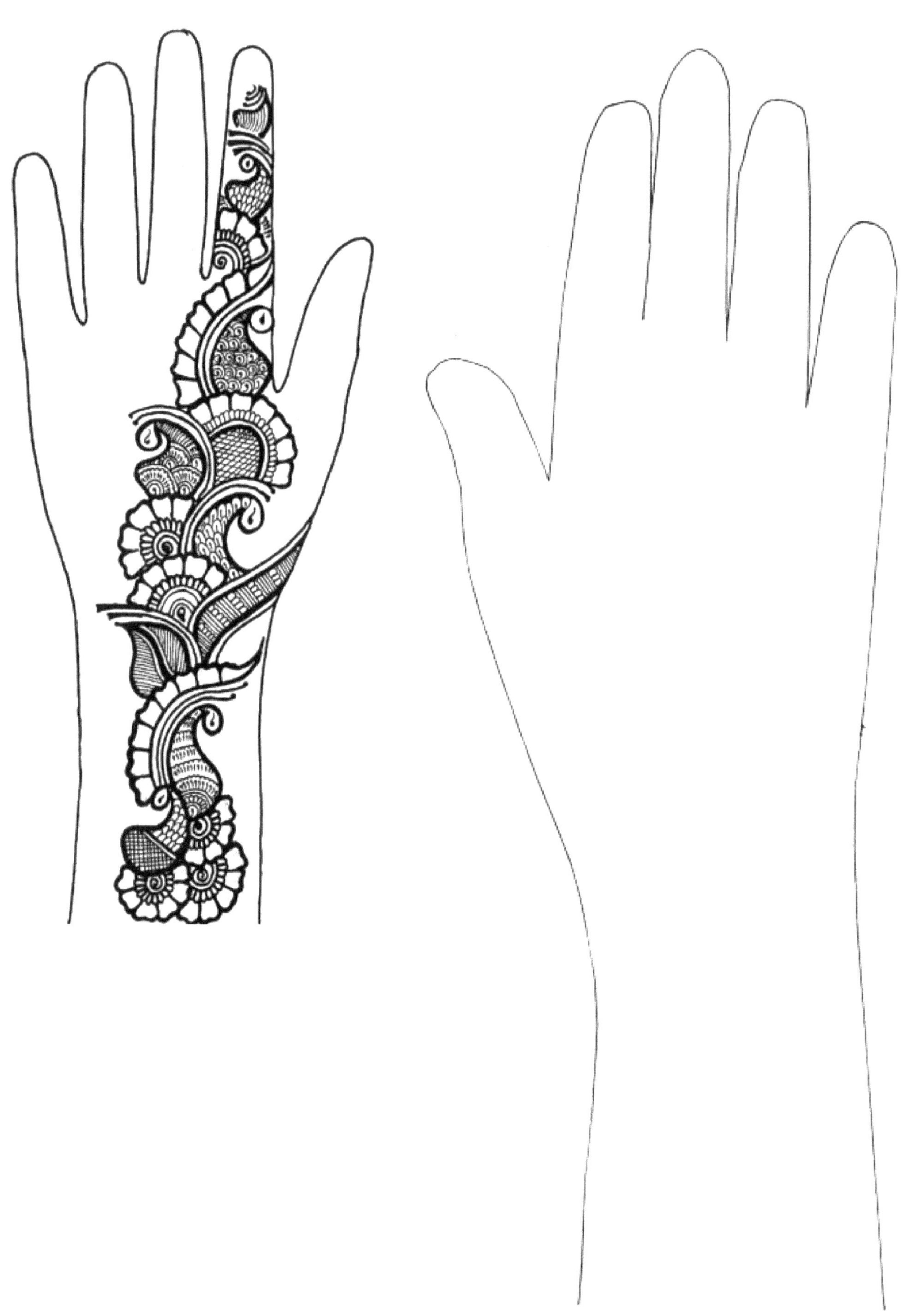

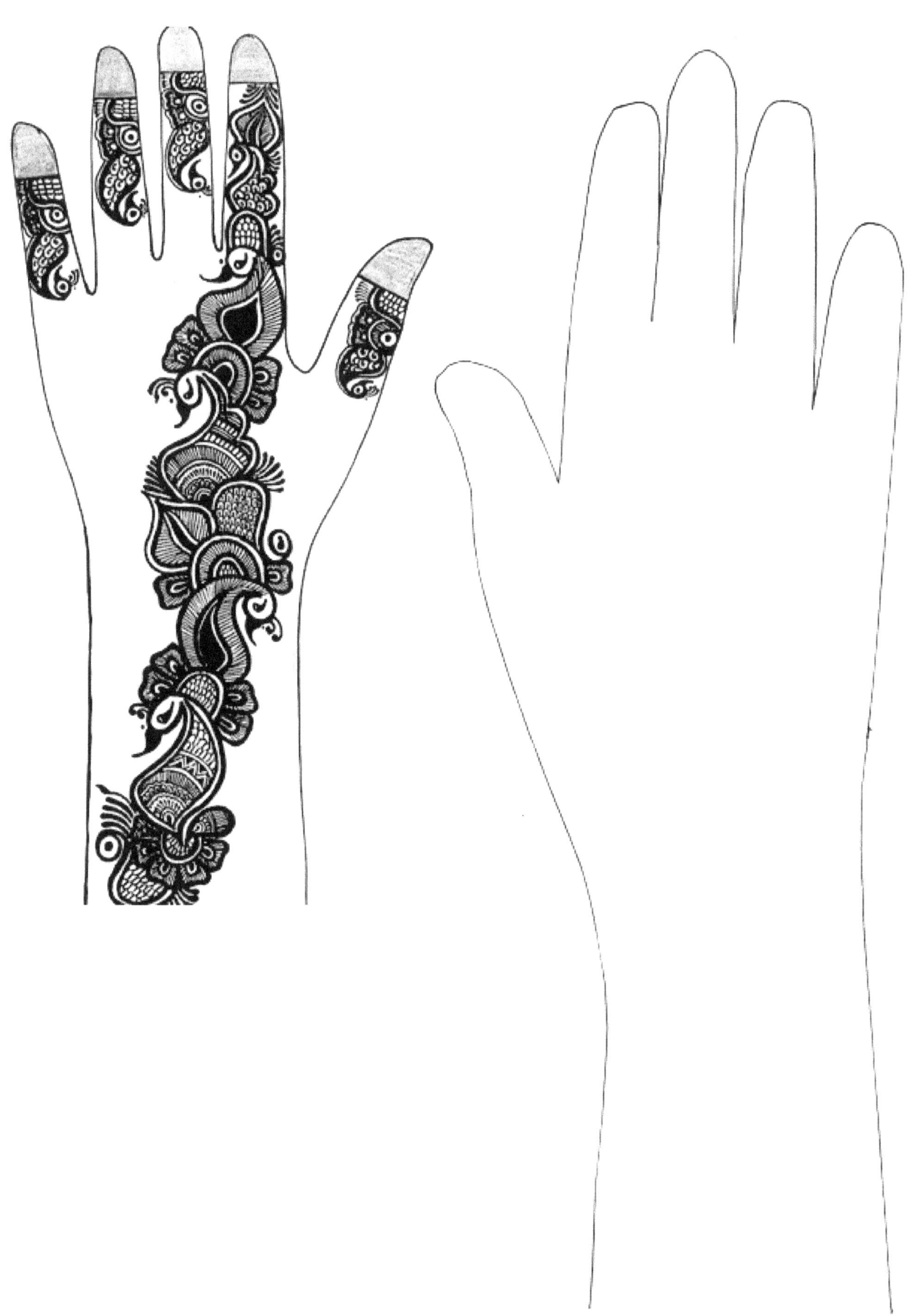

29

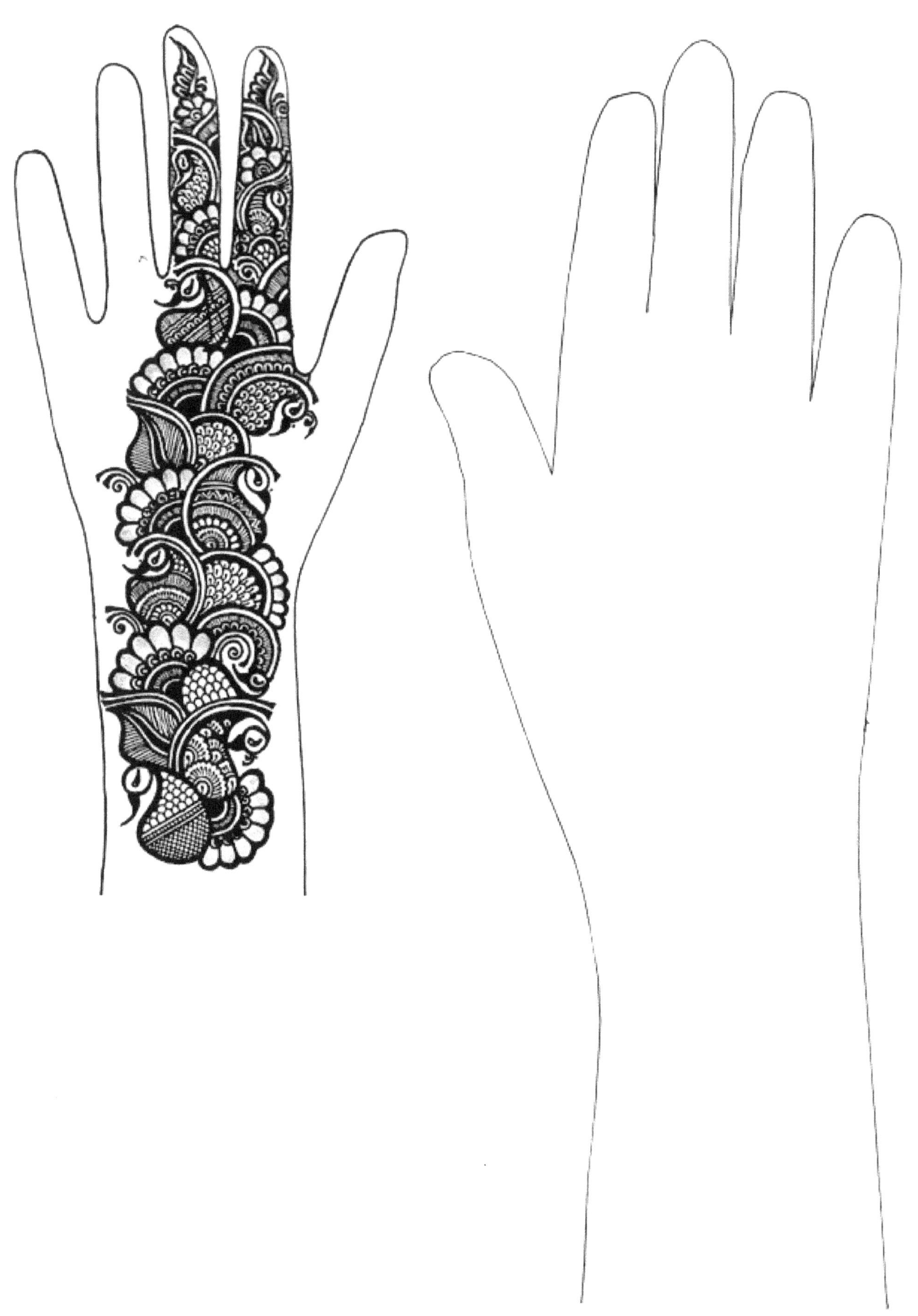

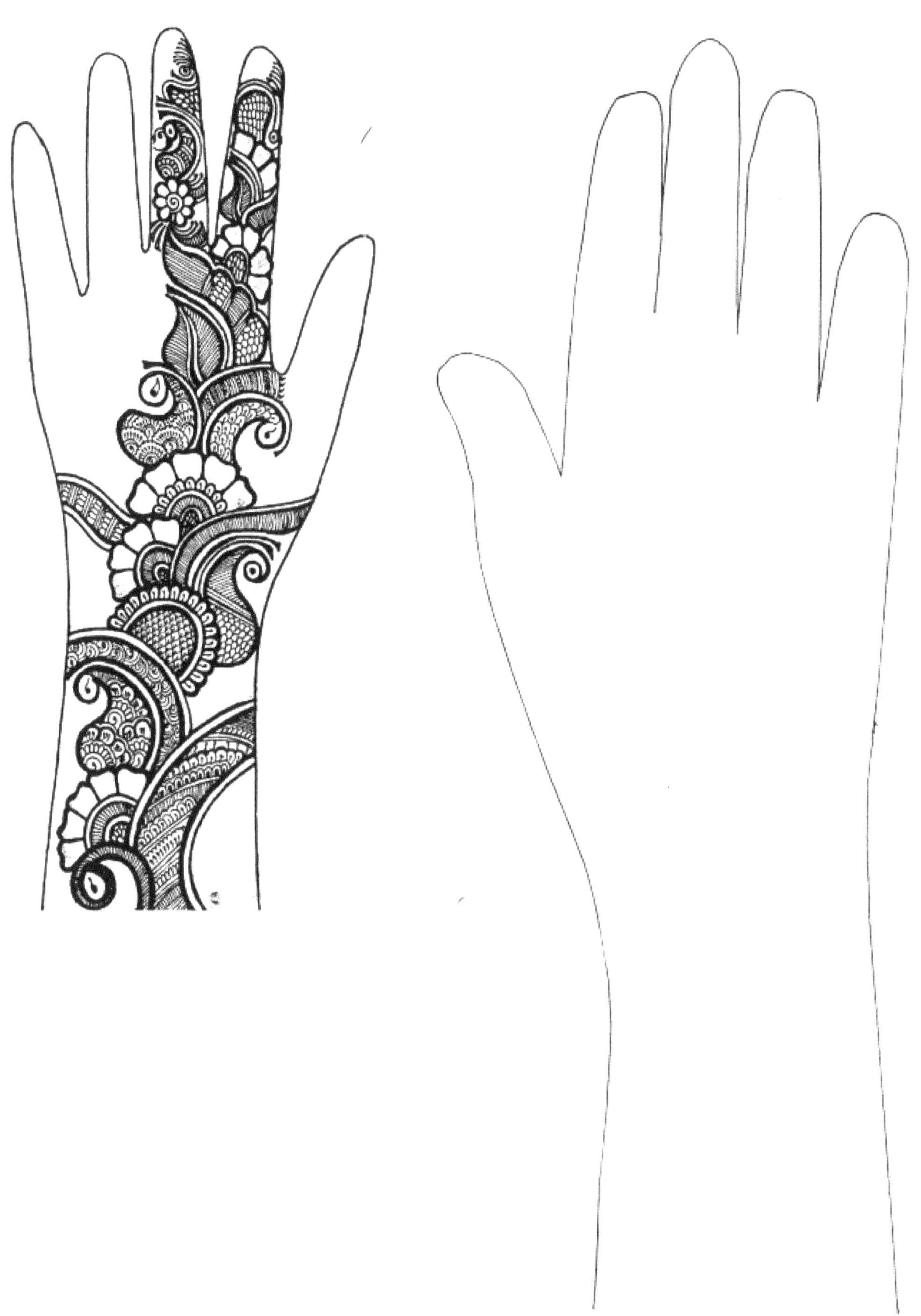

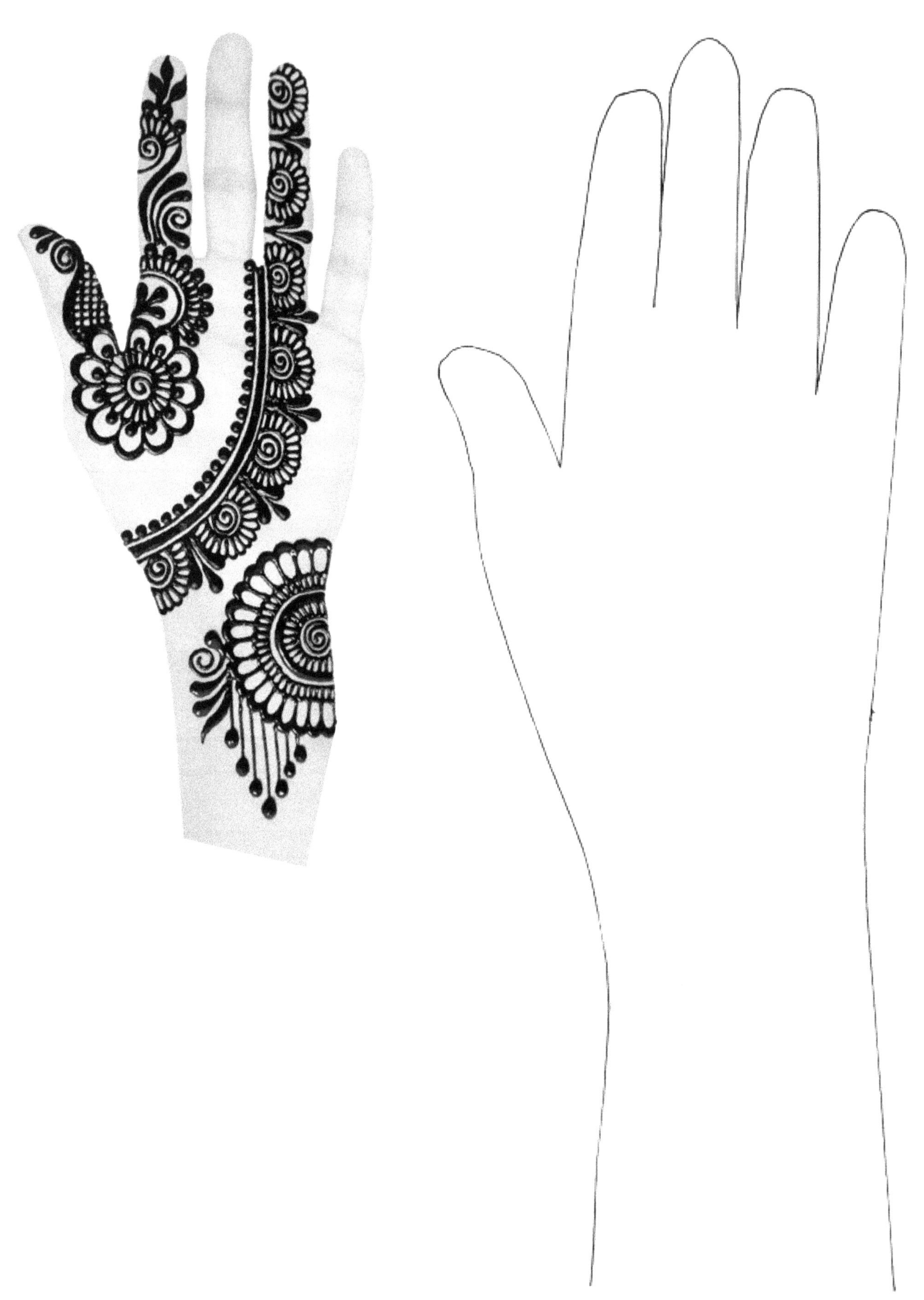

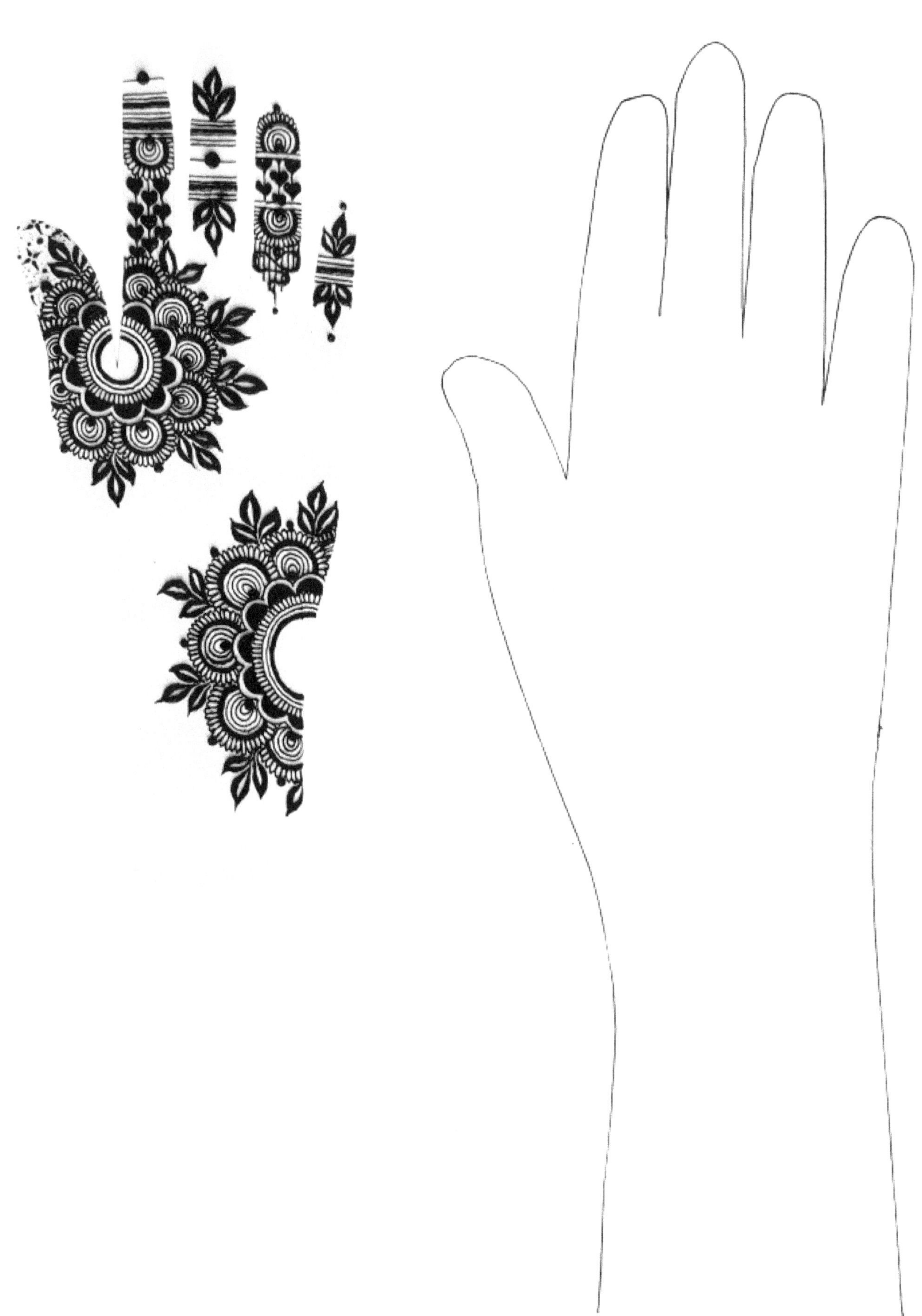

33

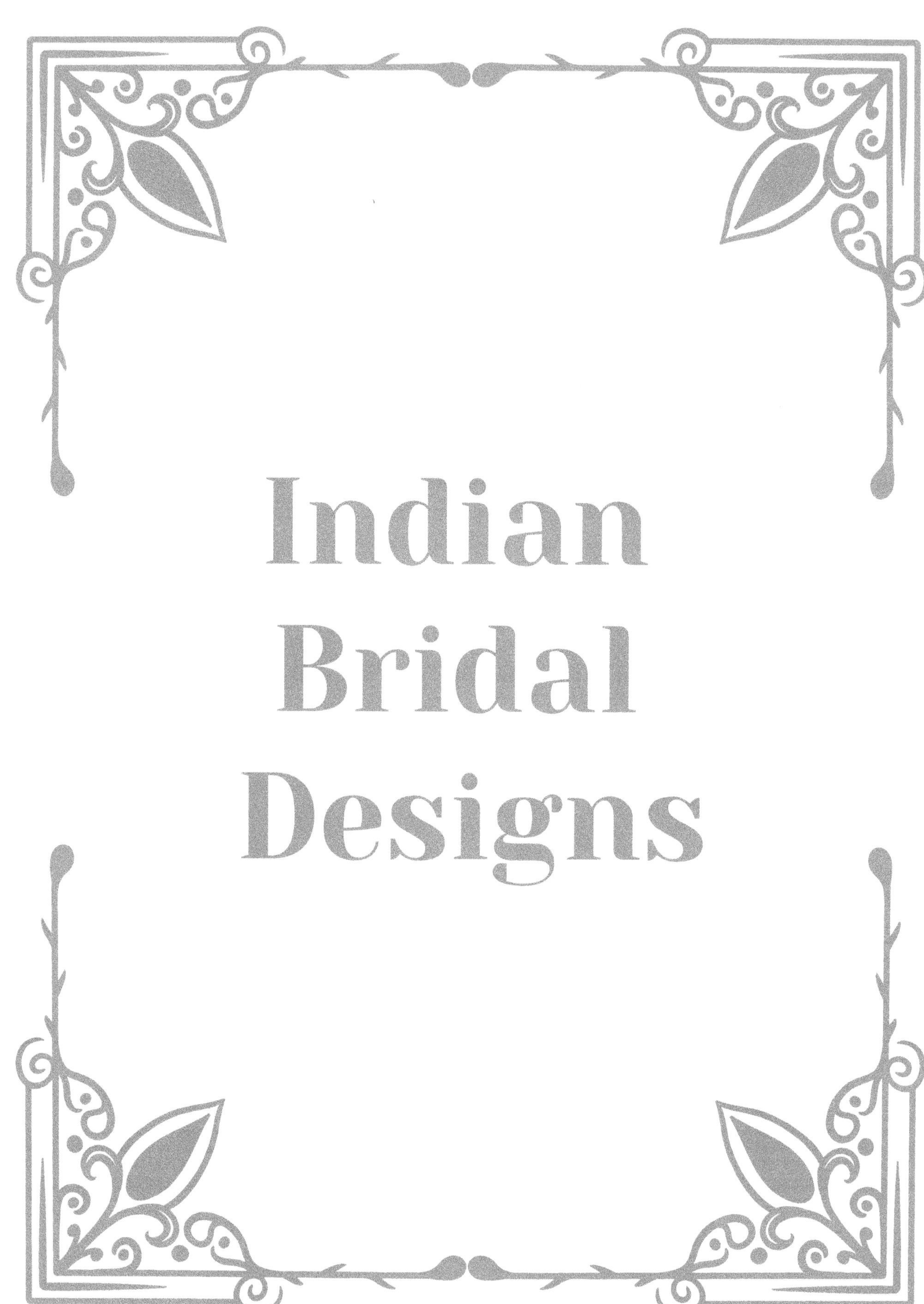

Indian
Bridal
Designs

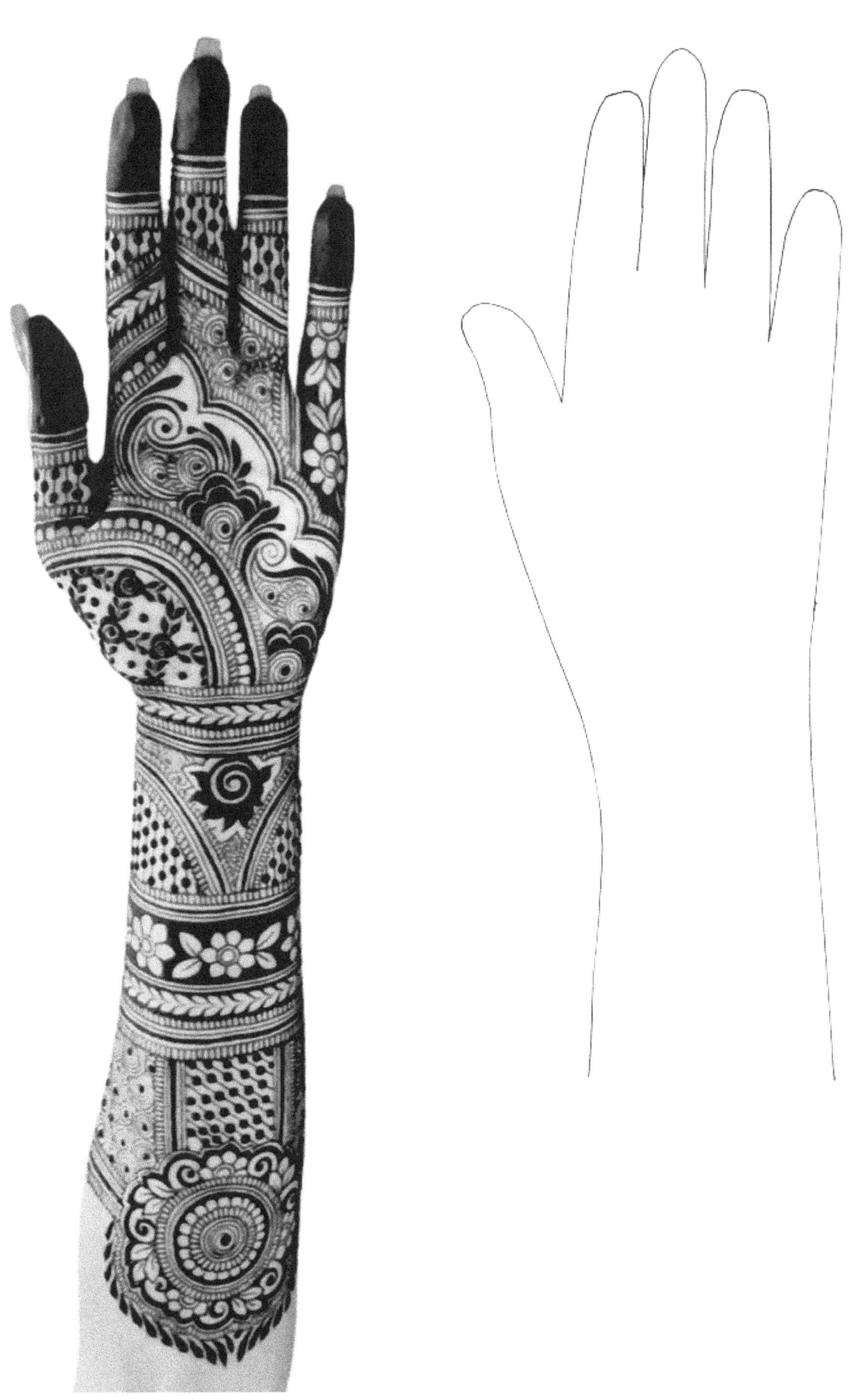

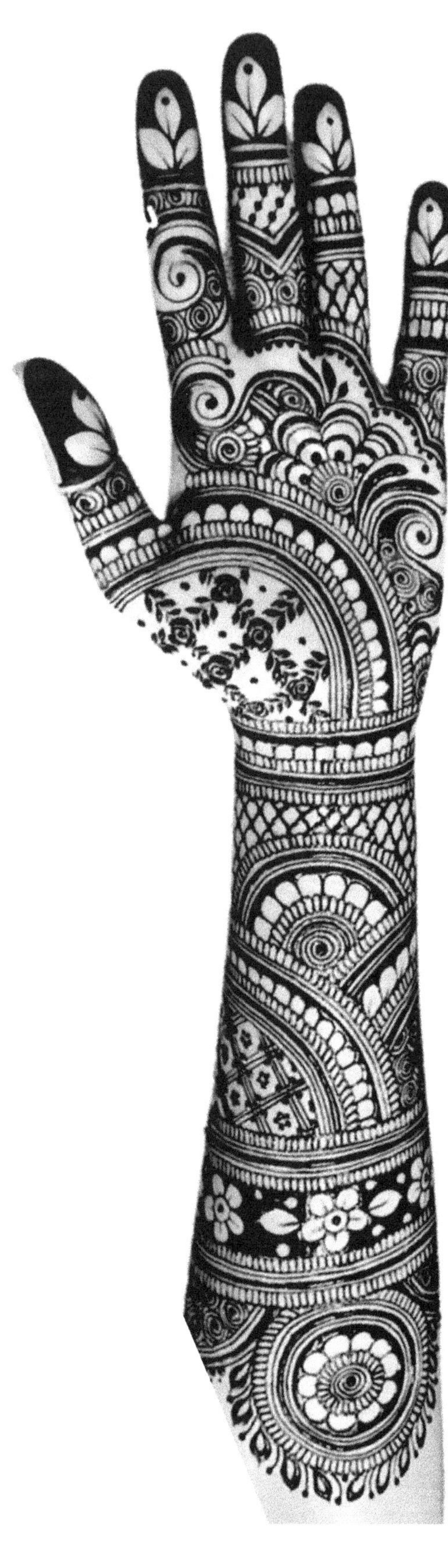
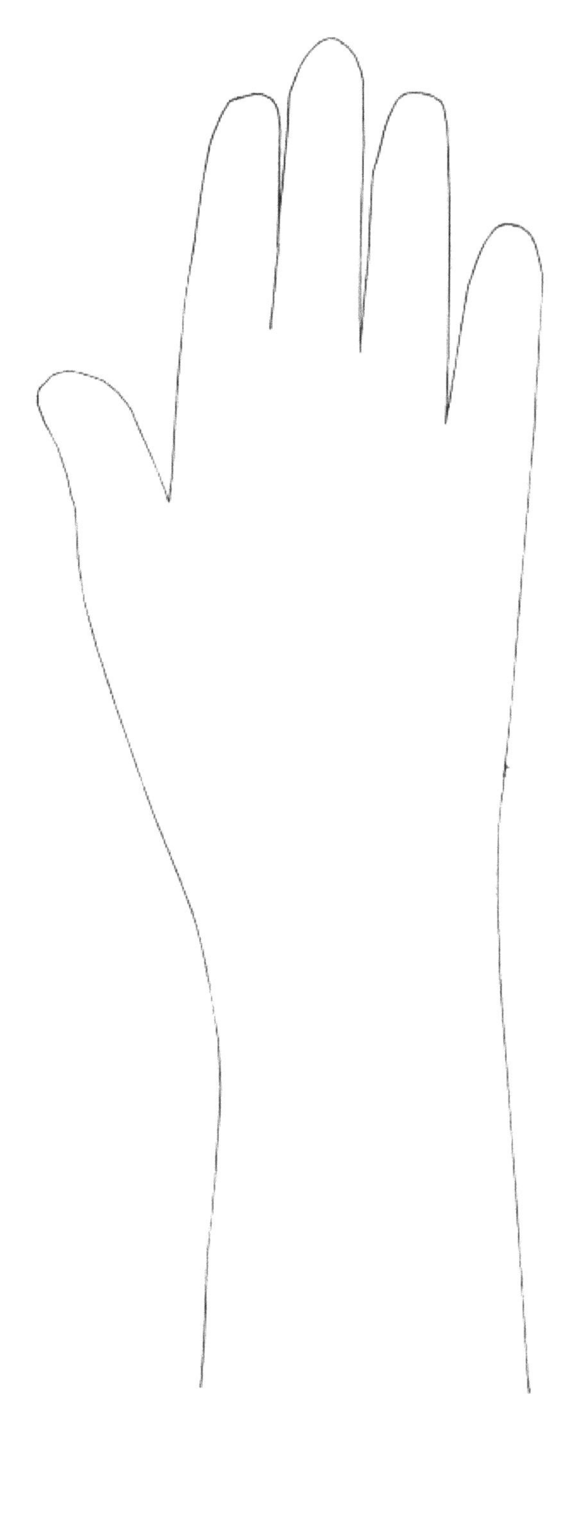

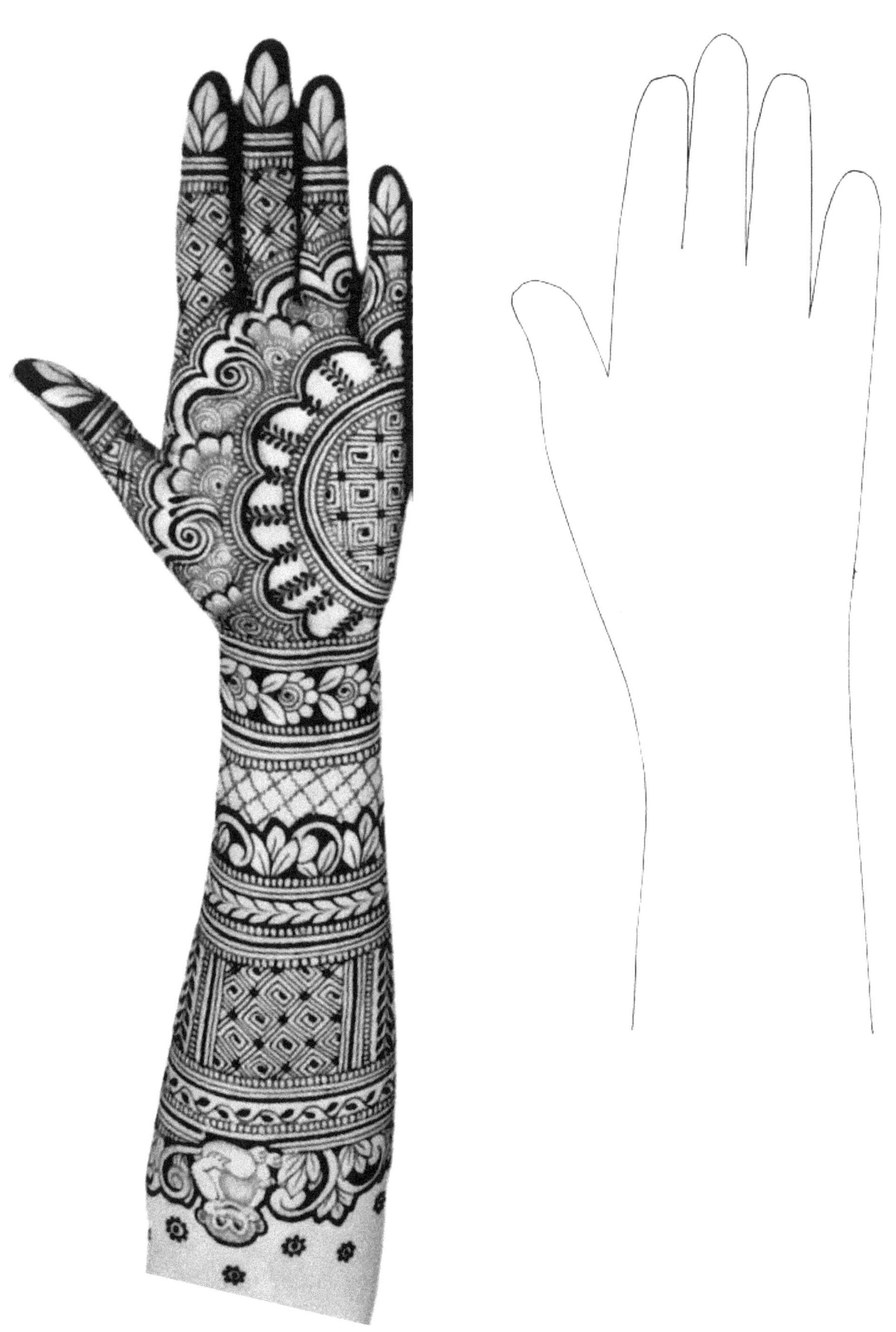

37

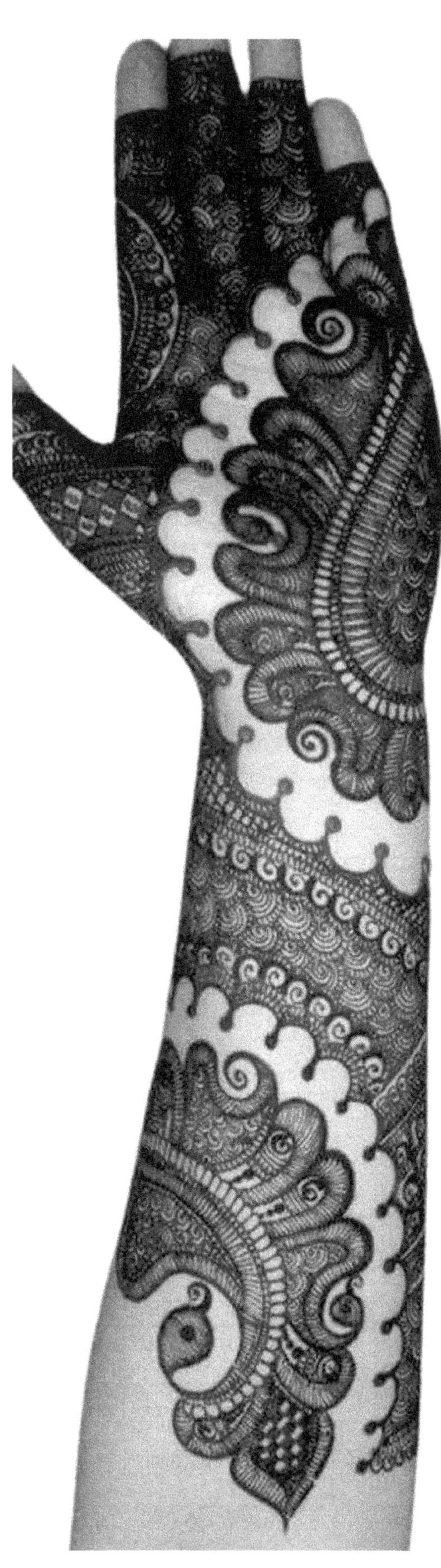
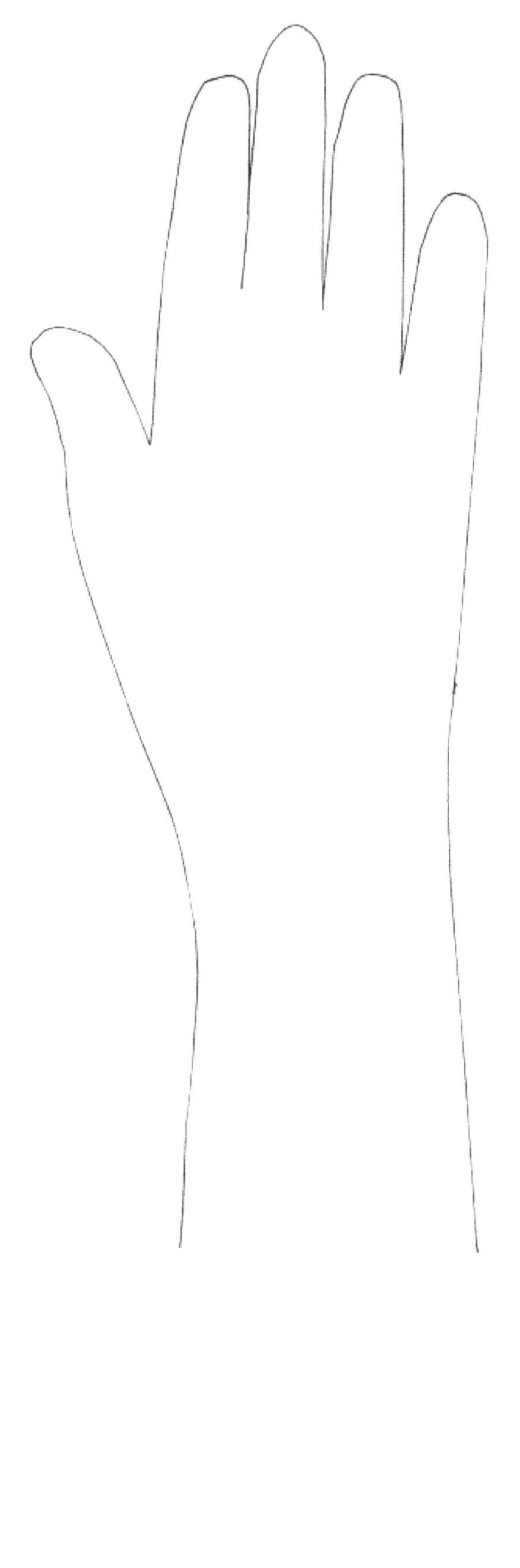

38

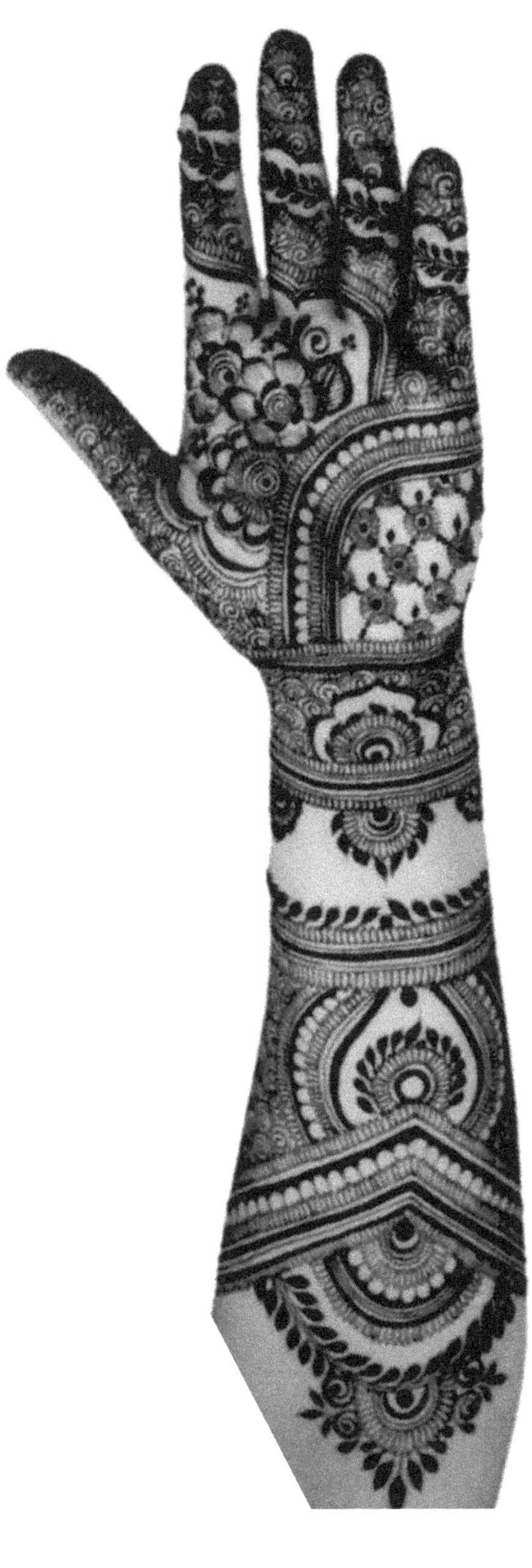
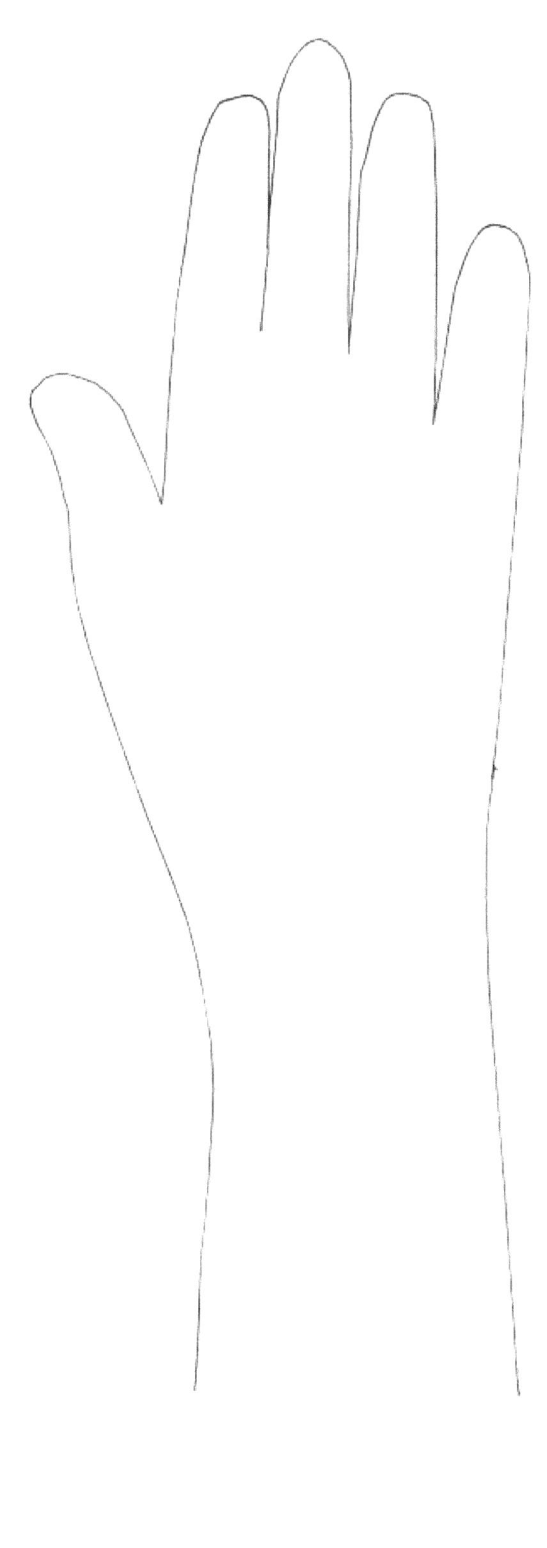

39

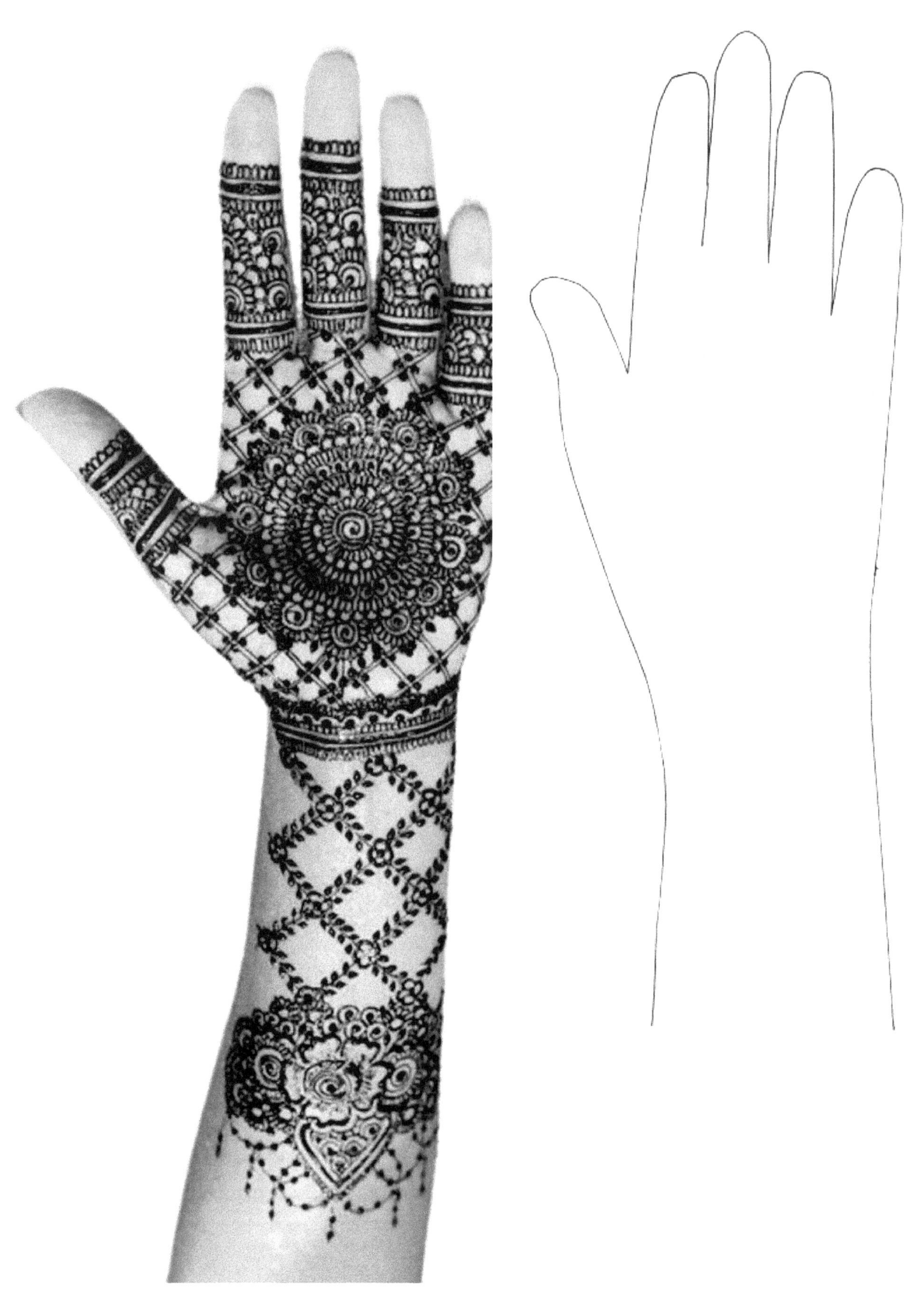

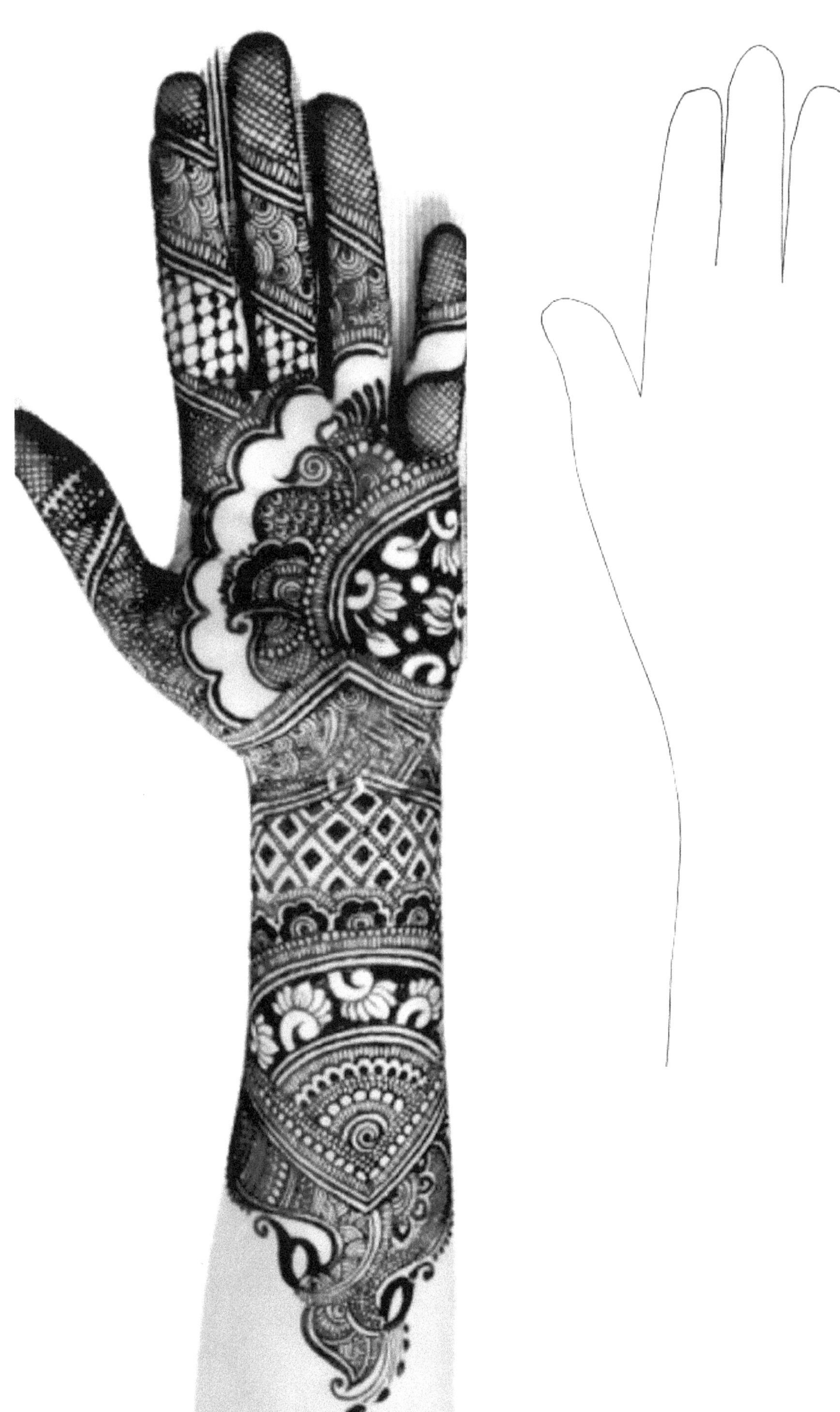

41

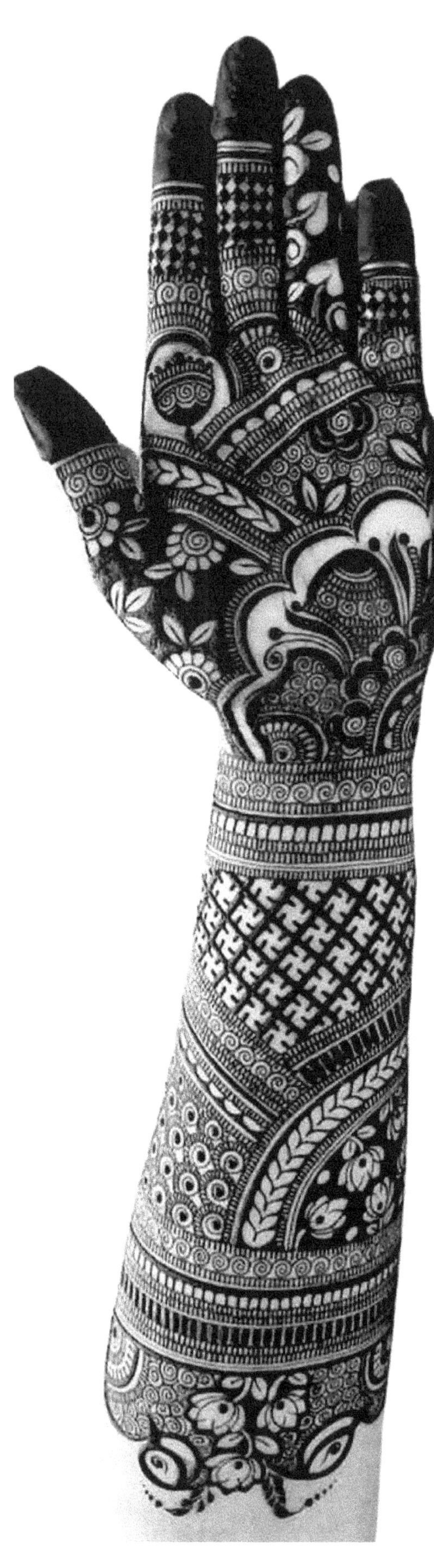
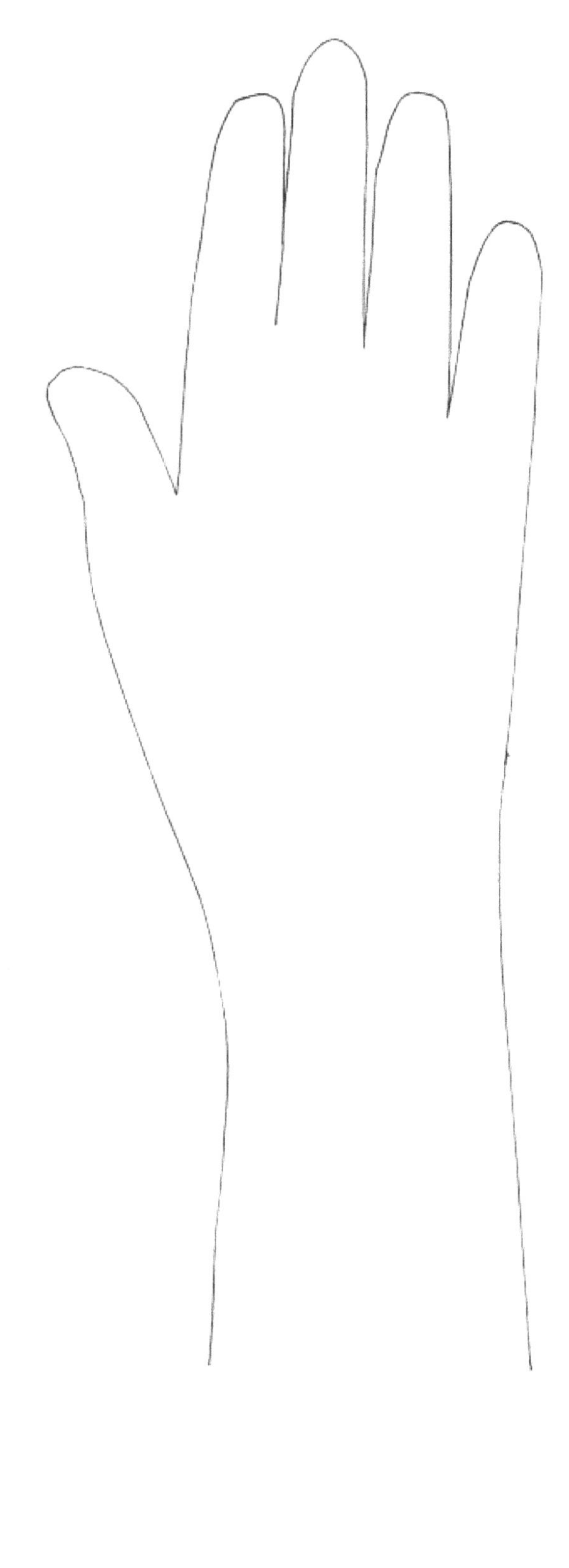

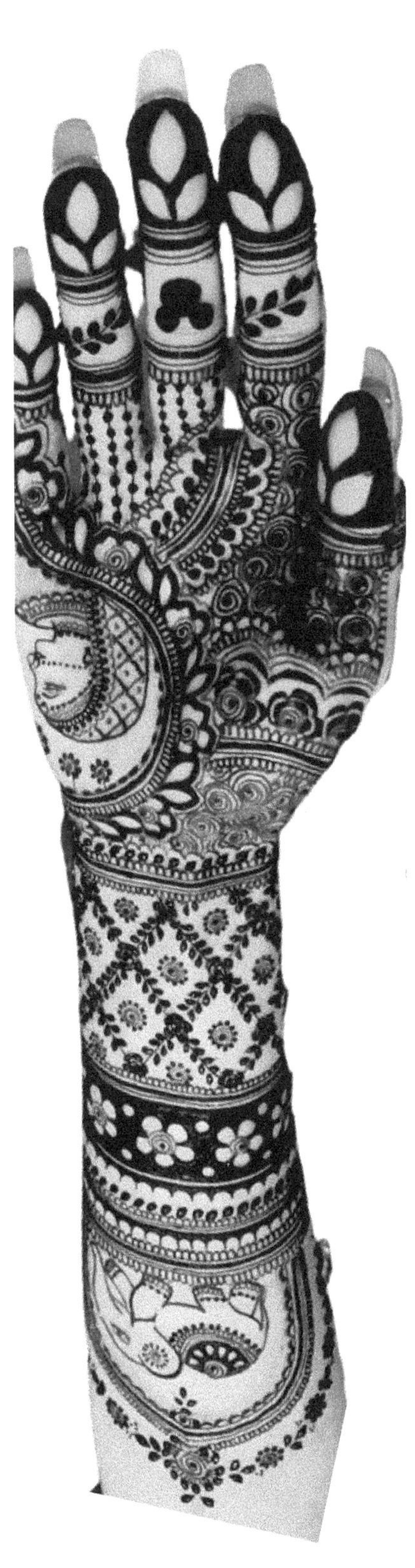
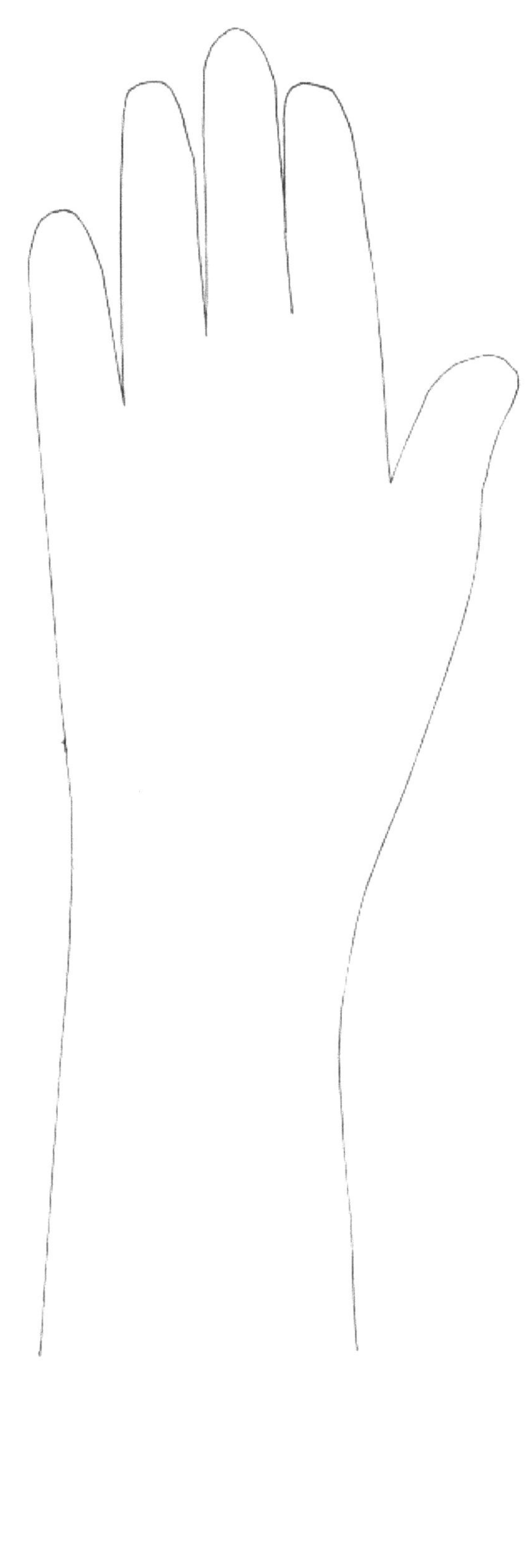

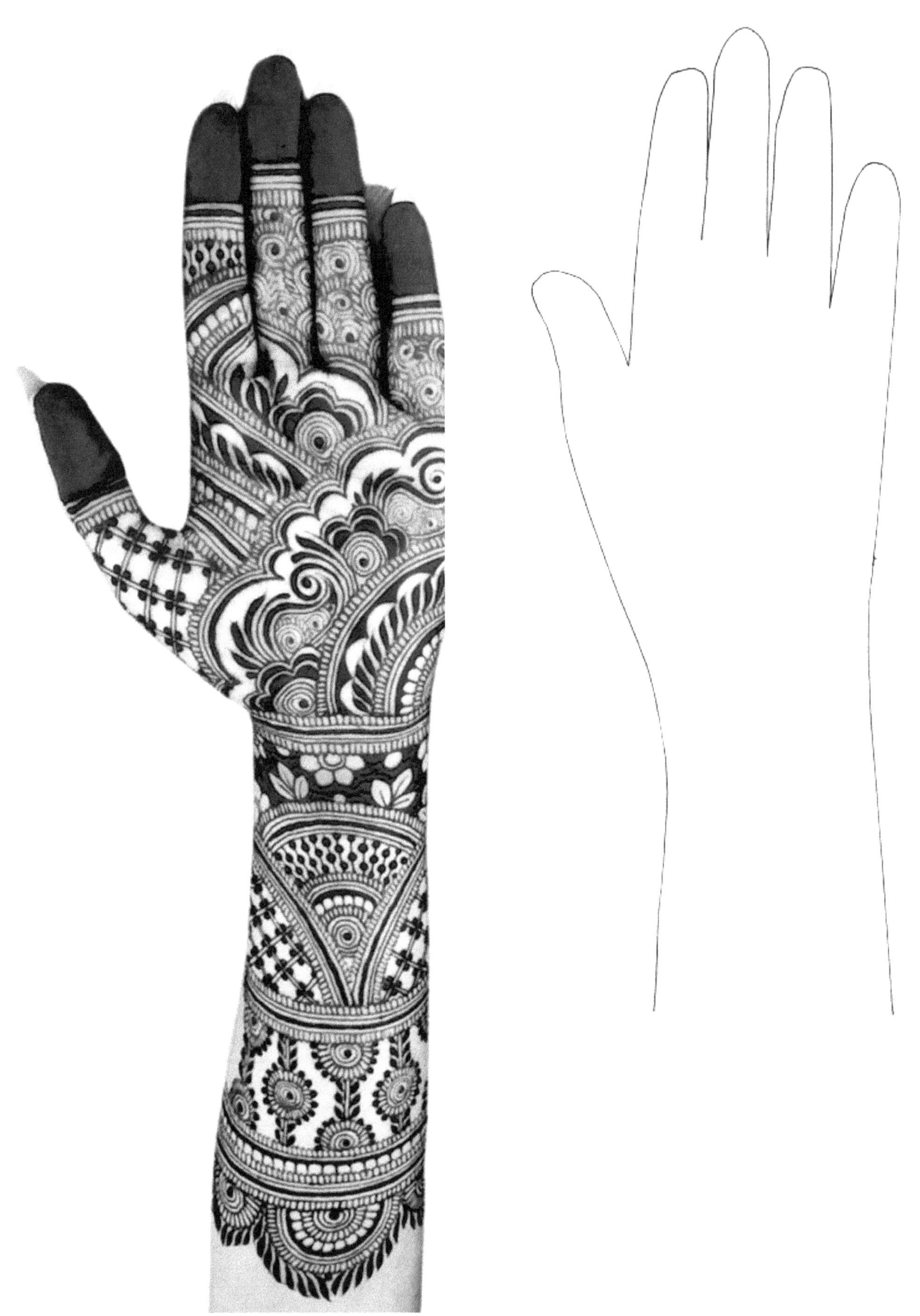

44

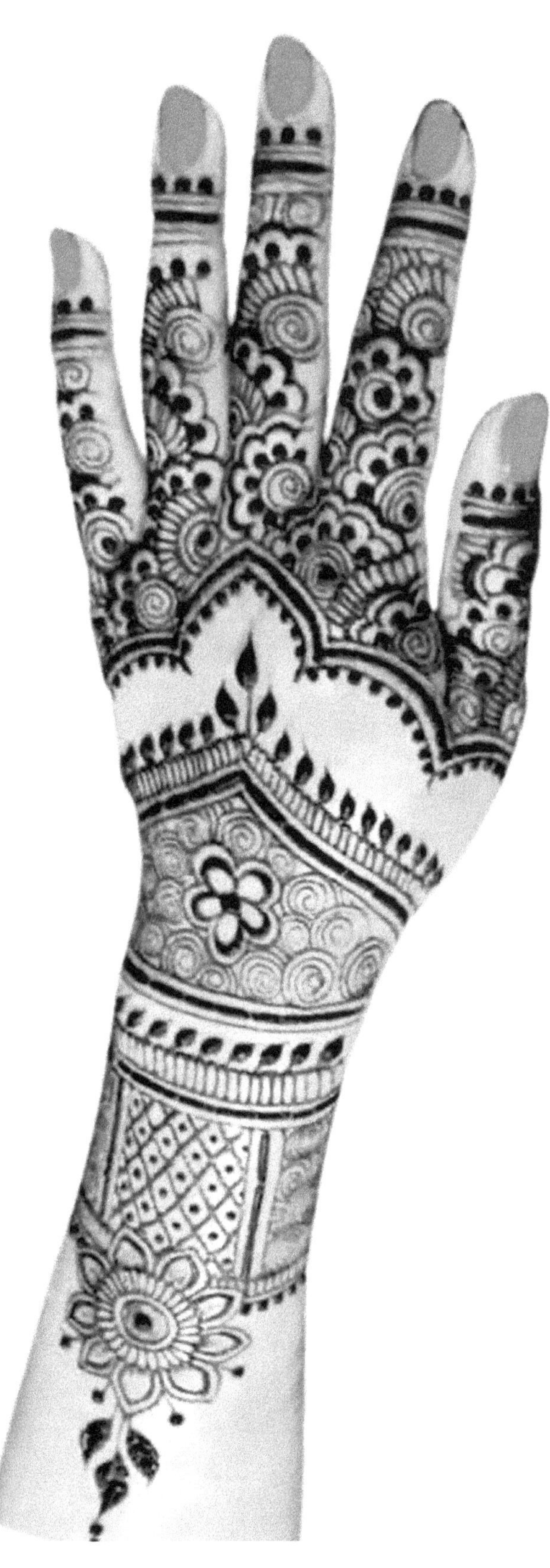

Feet Designs

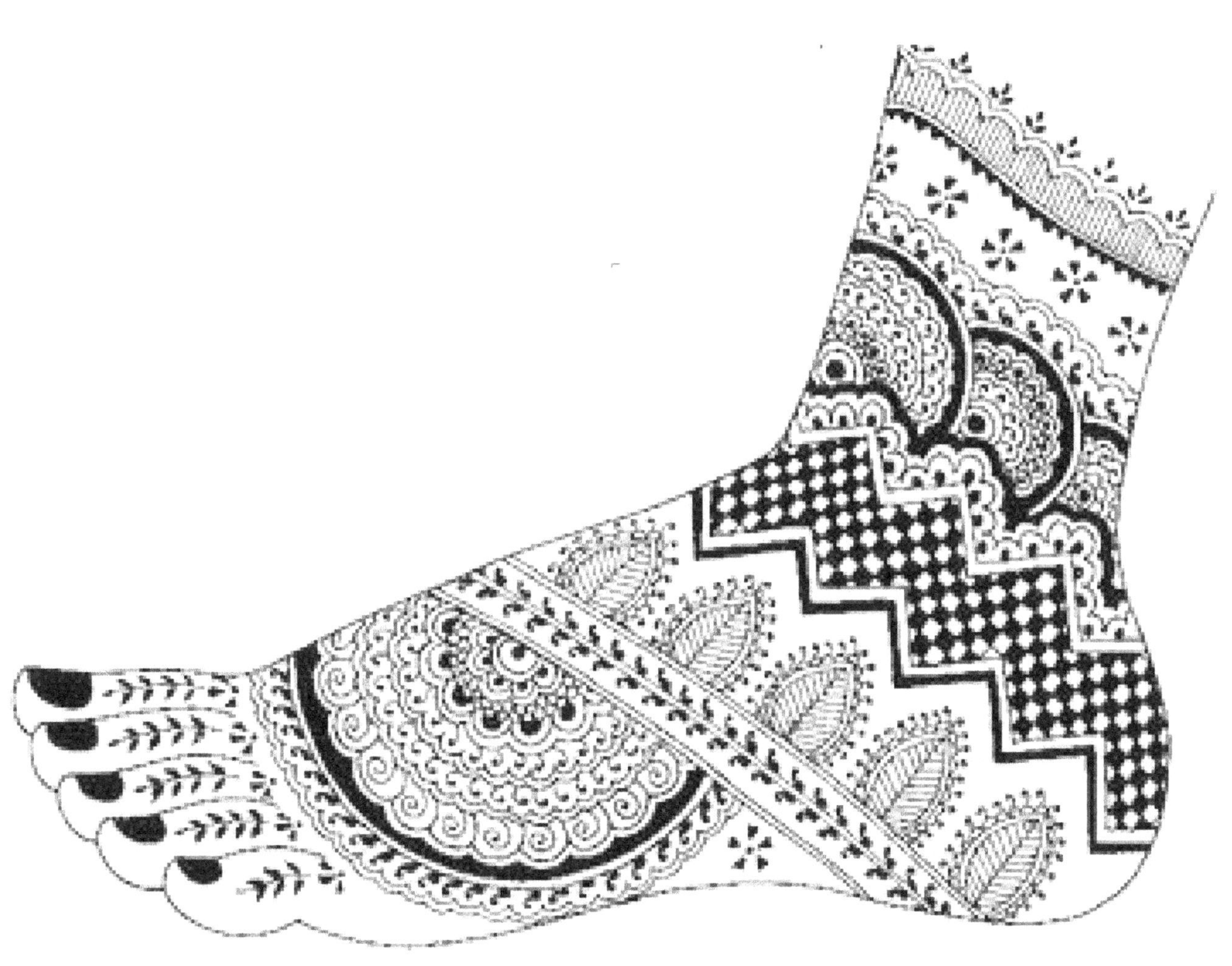

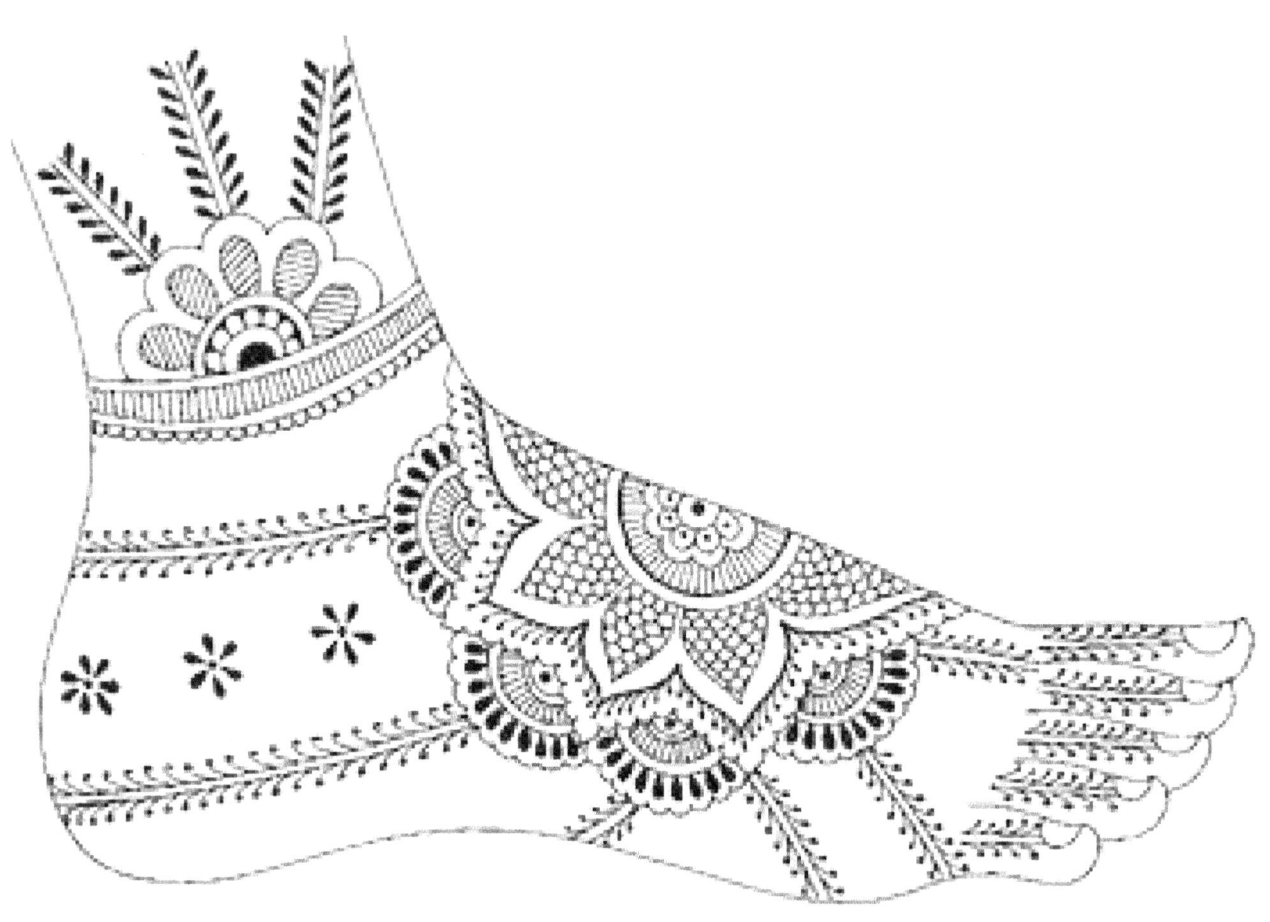

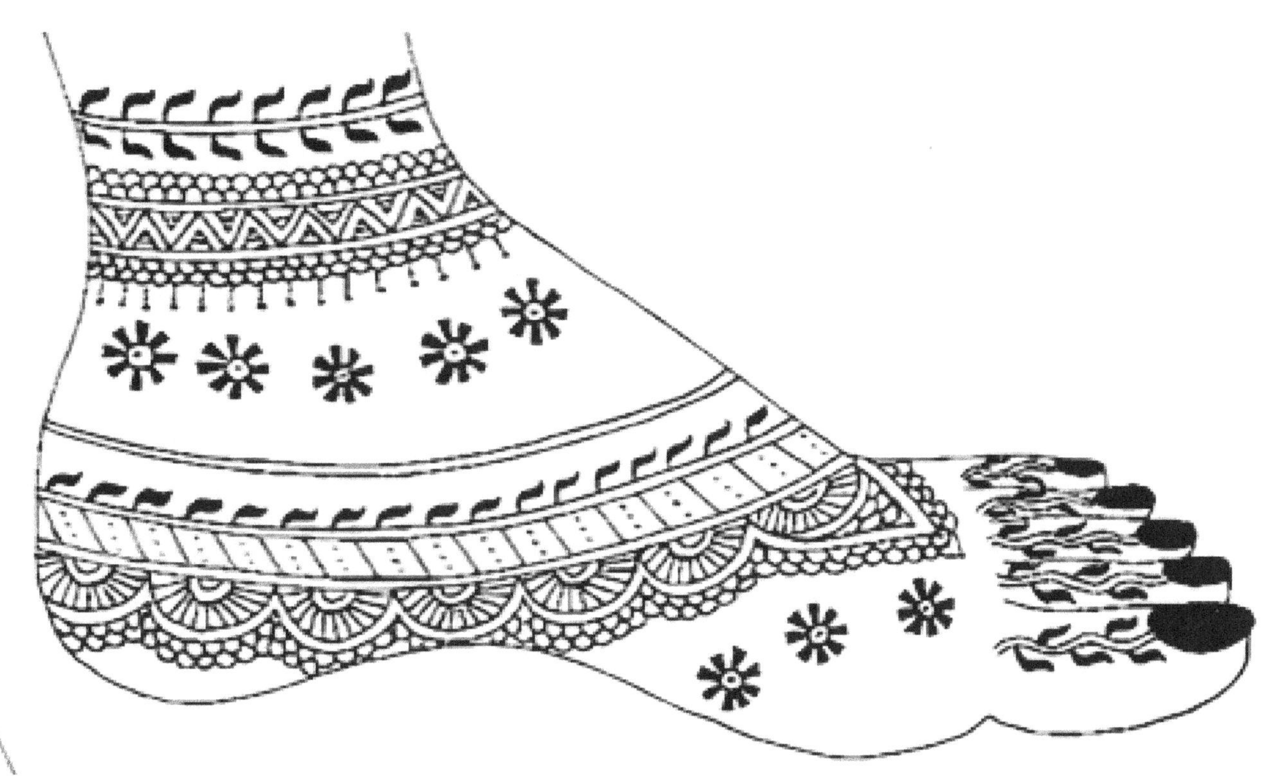

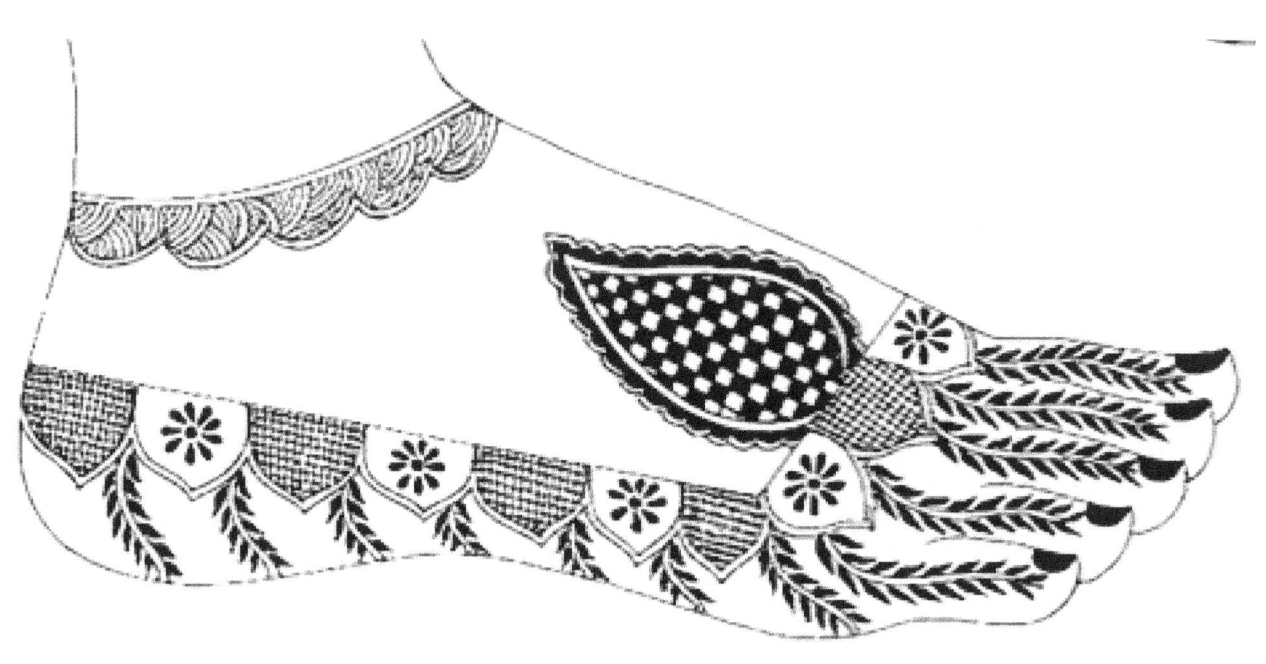

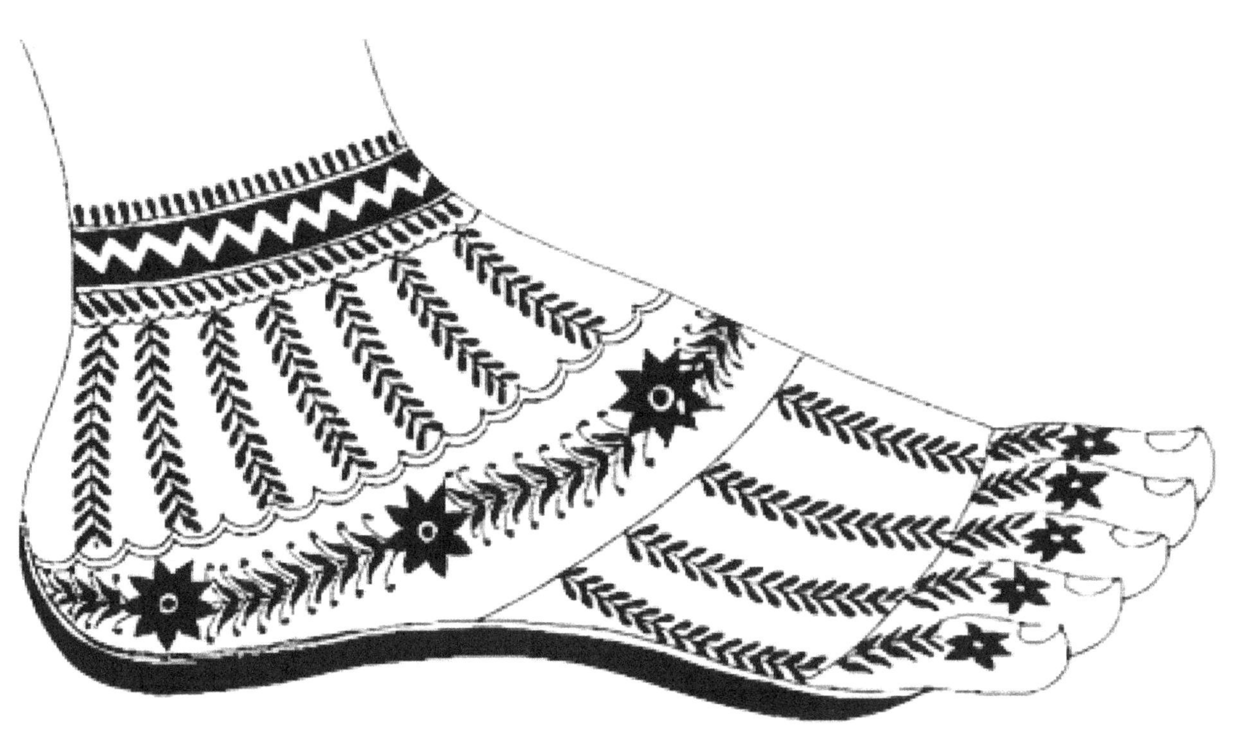

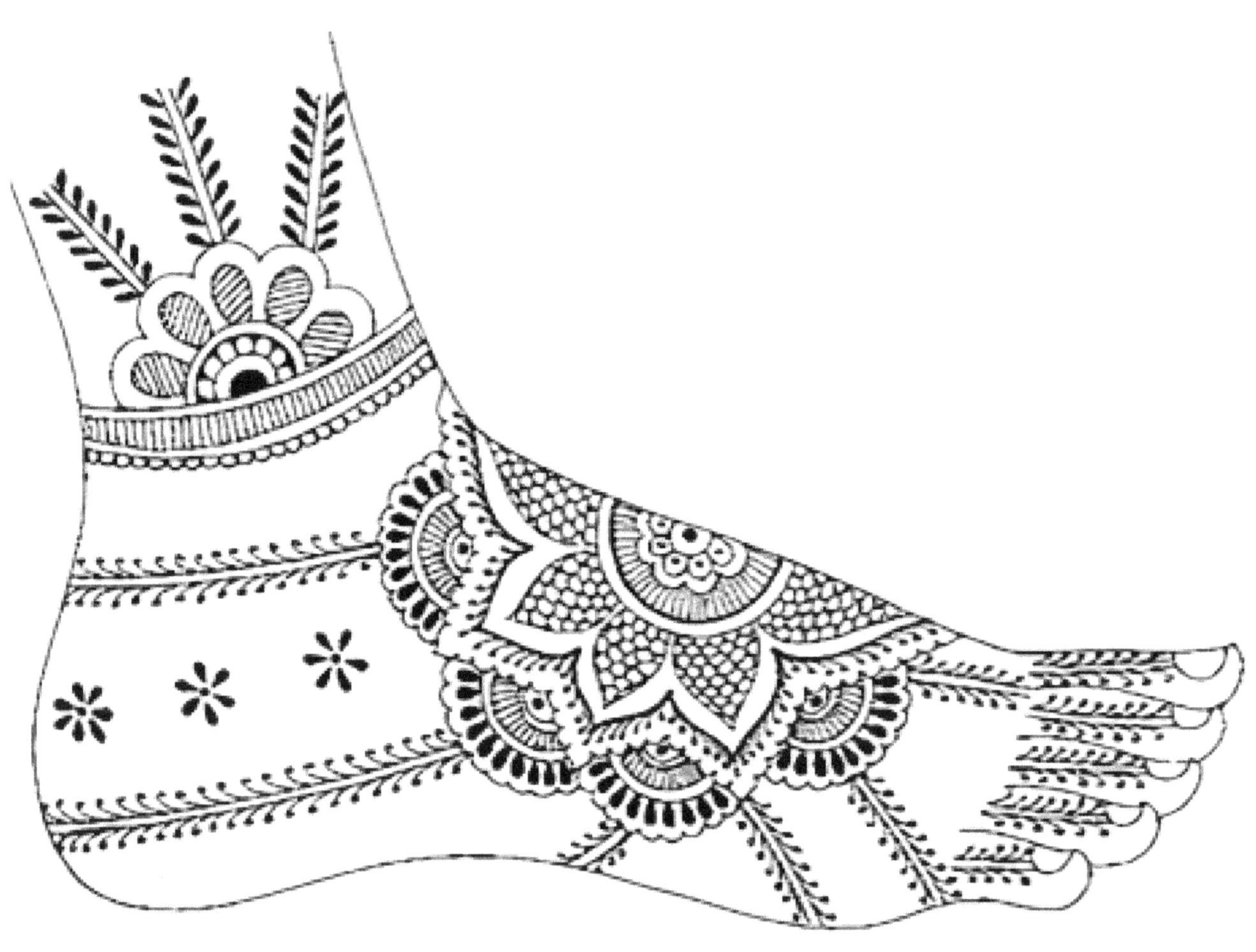

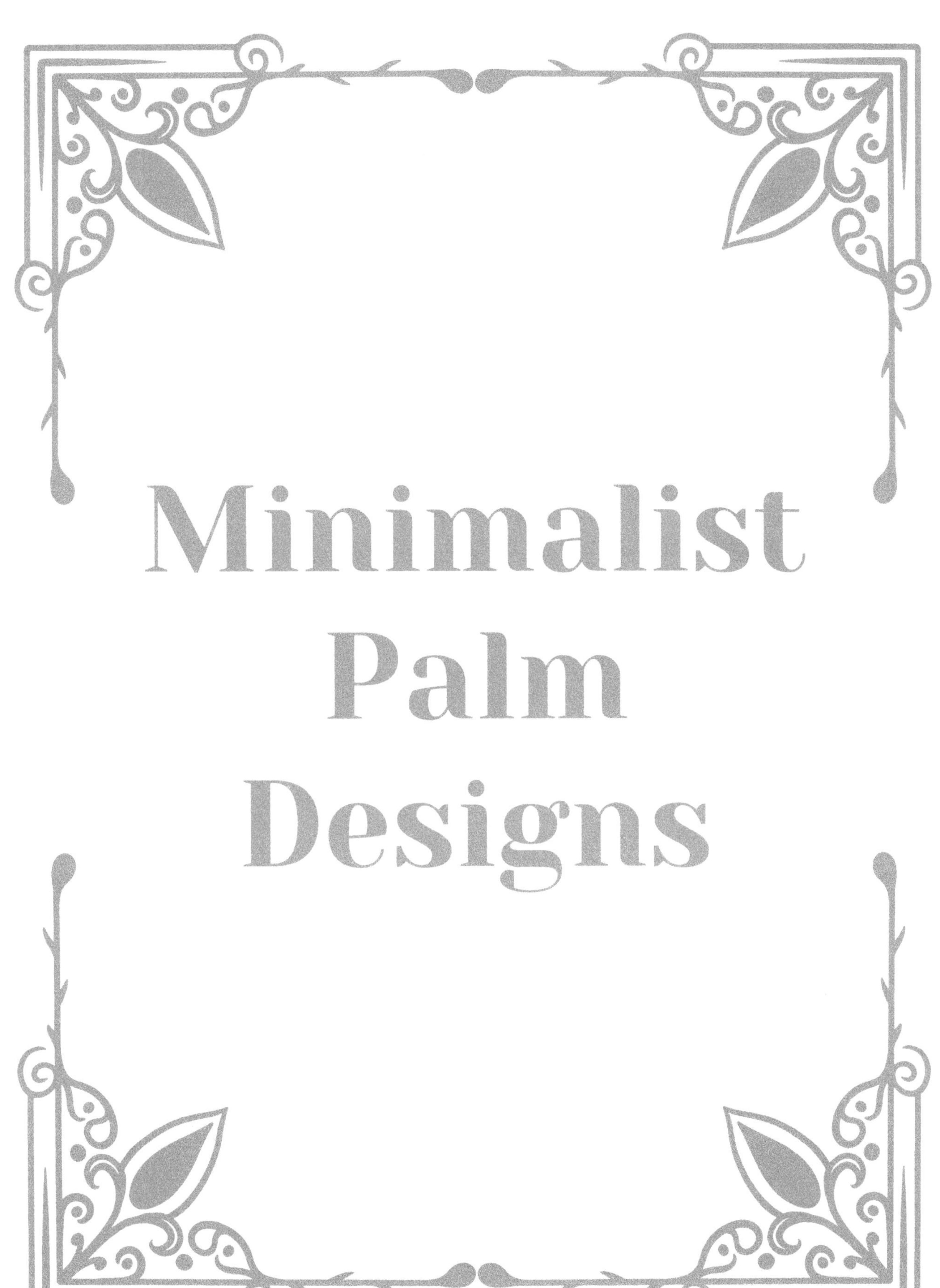

Minimalist Palm Designs

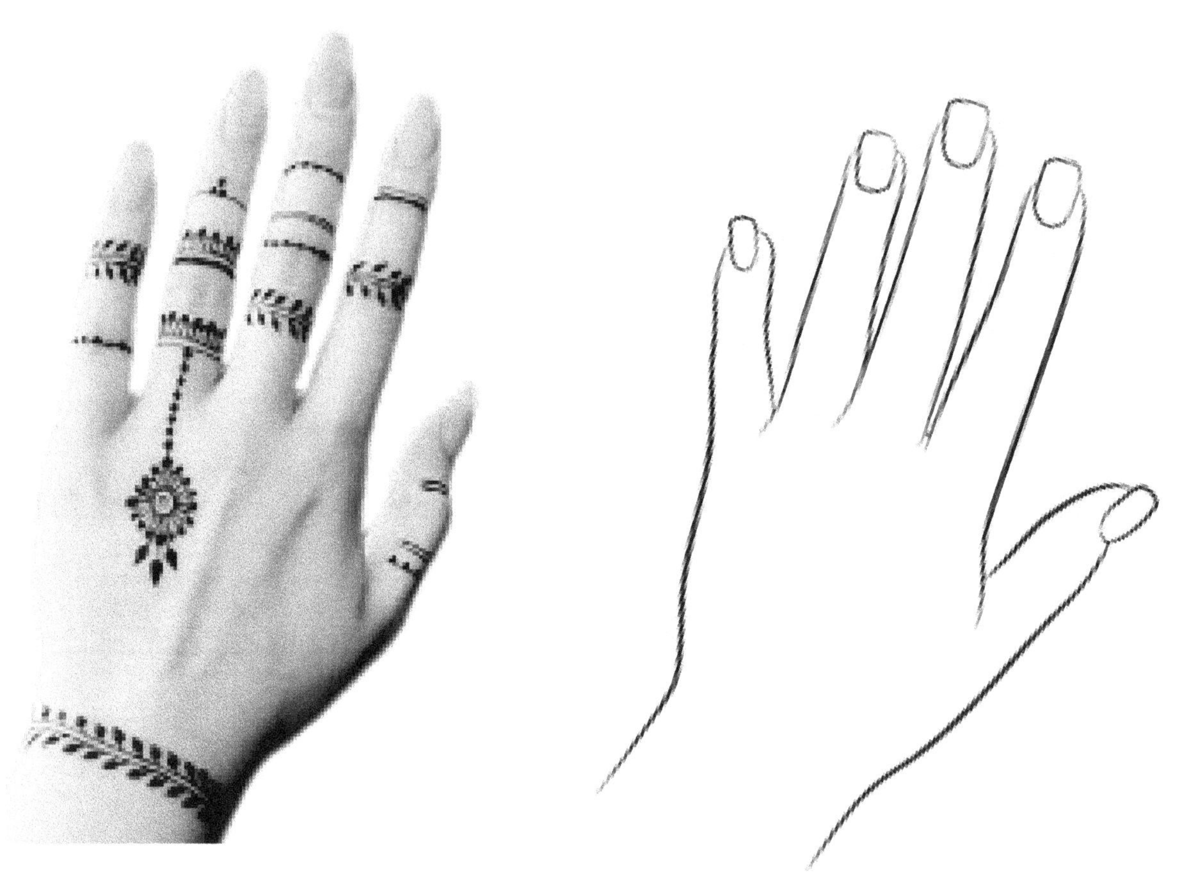

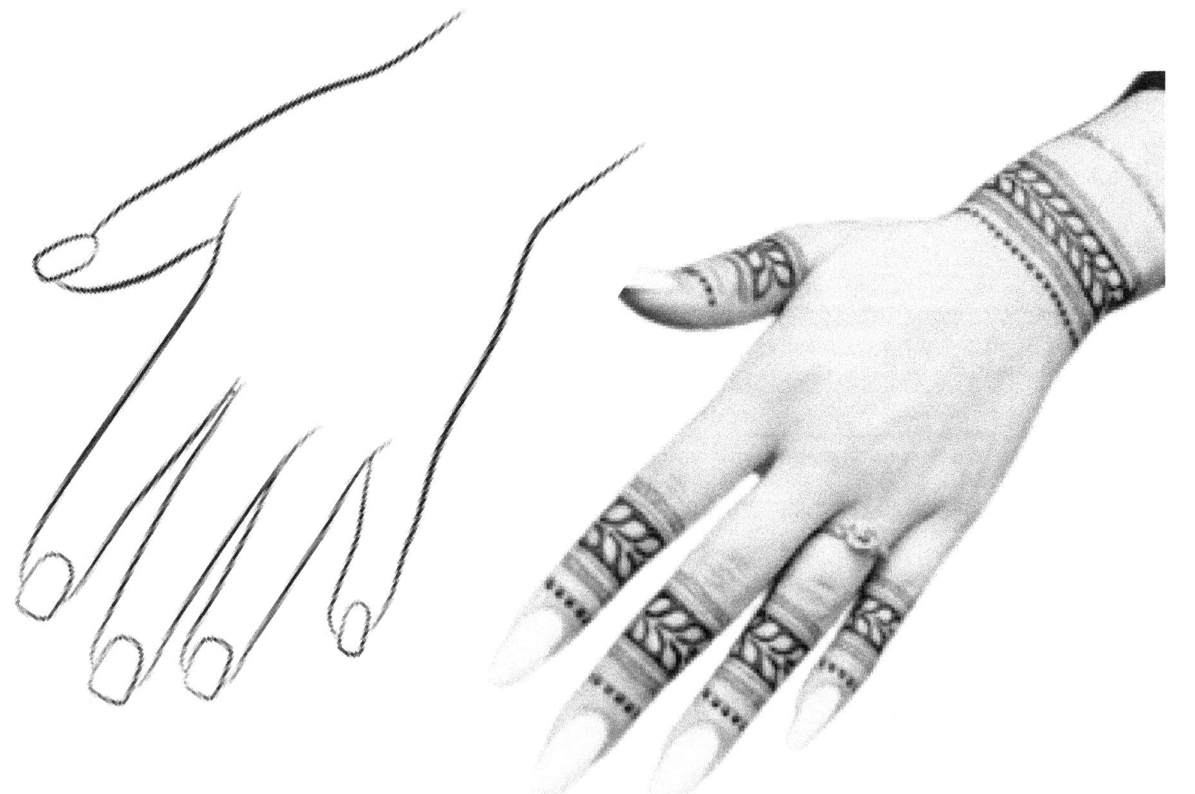

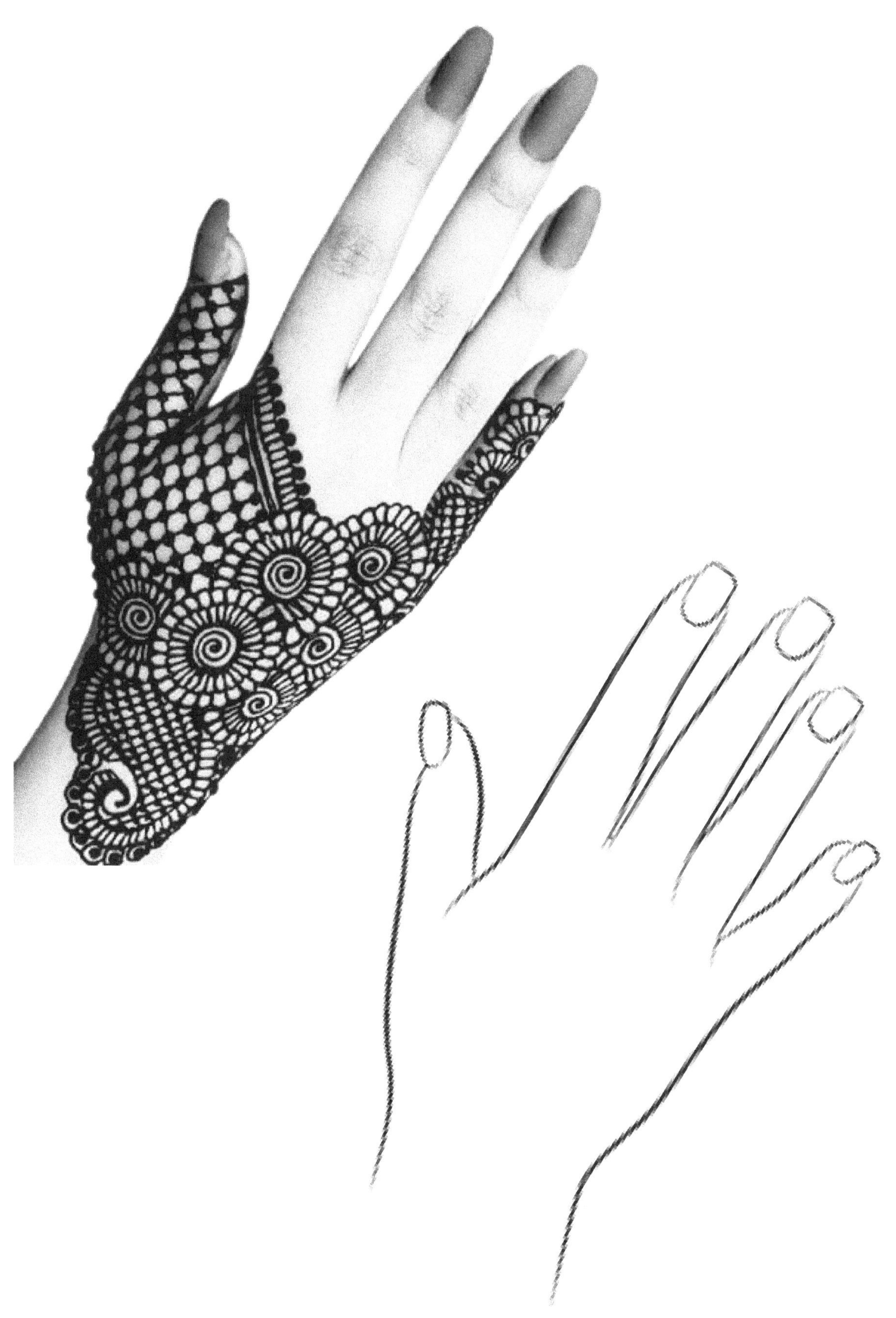

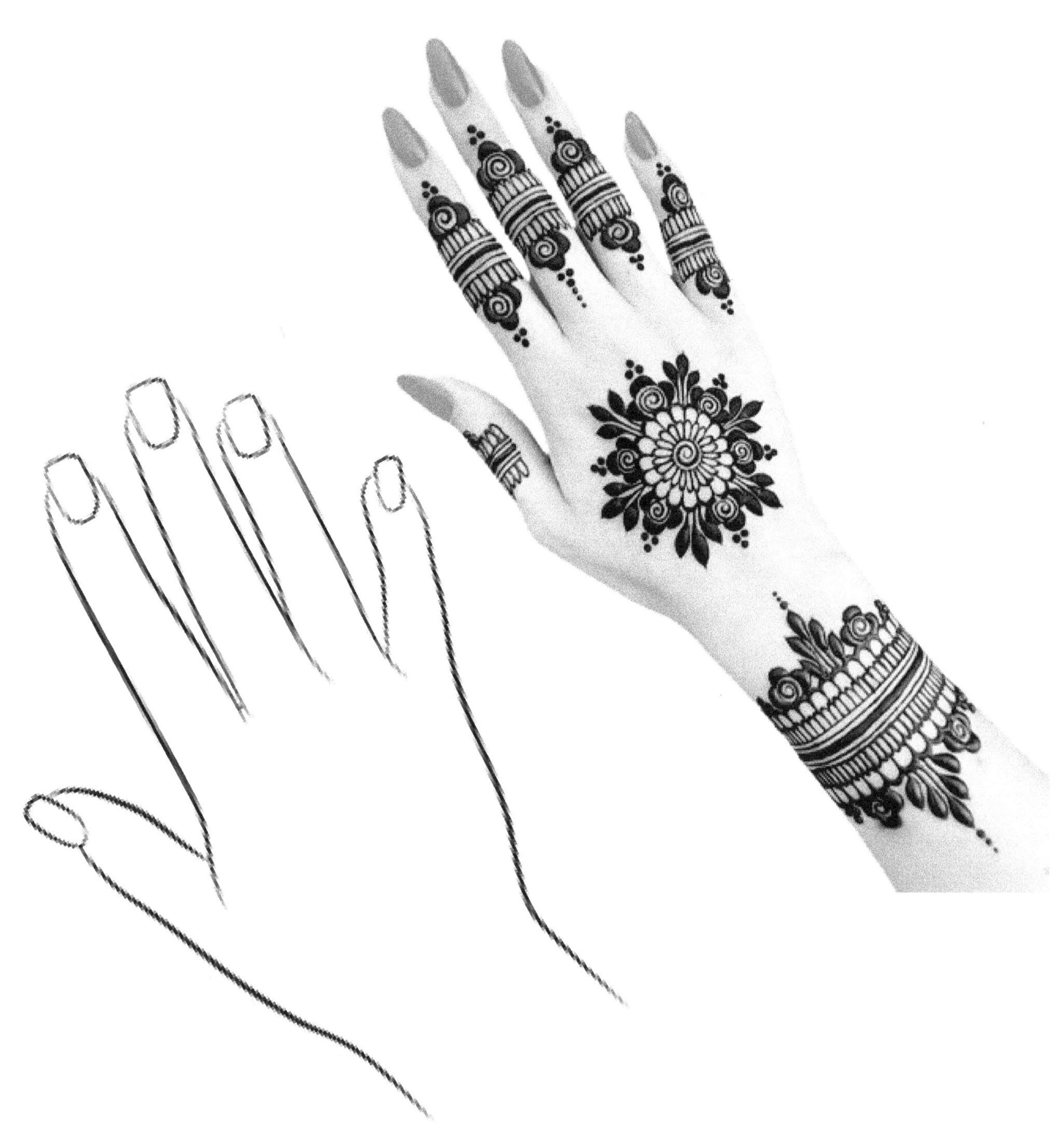

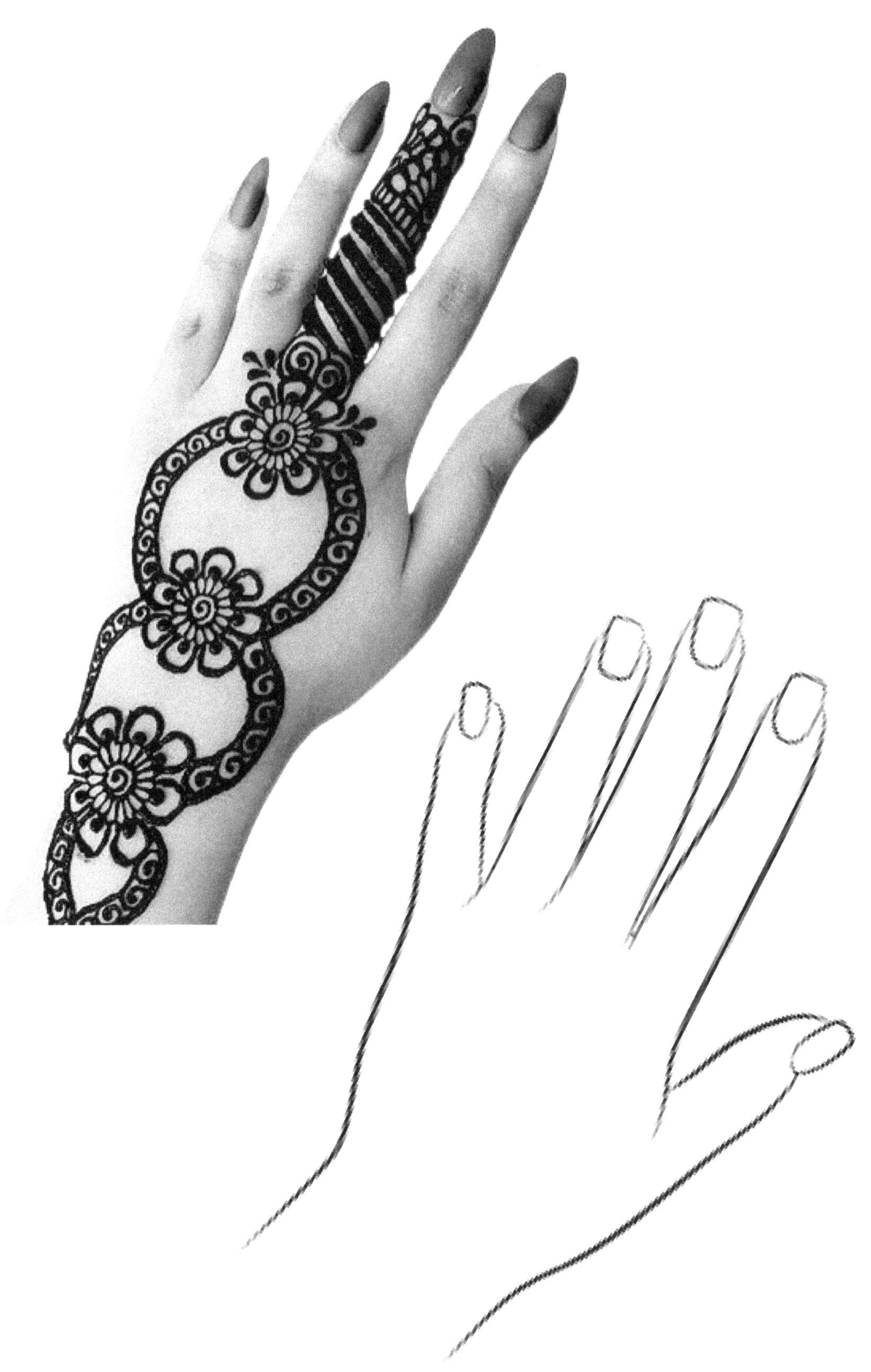

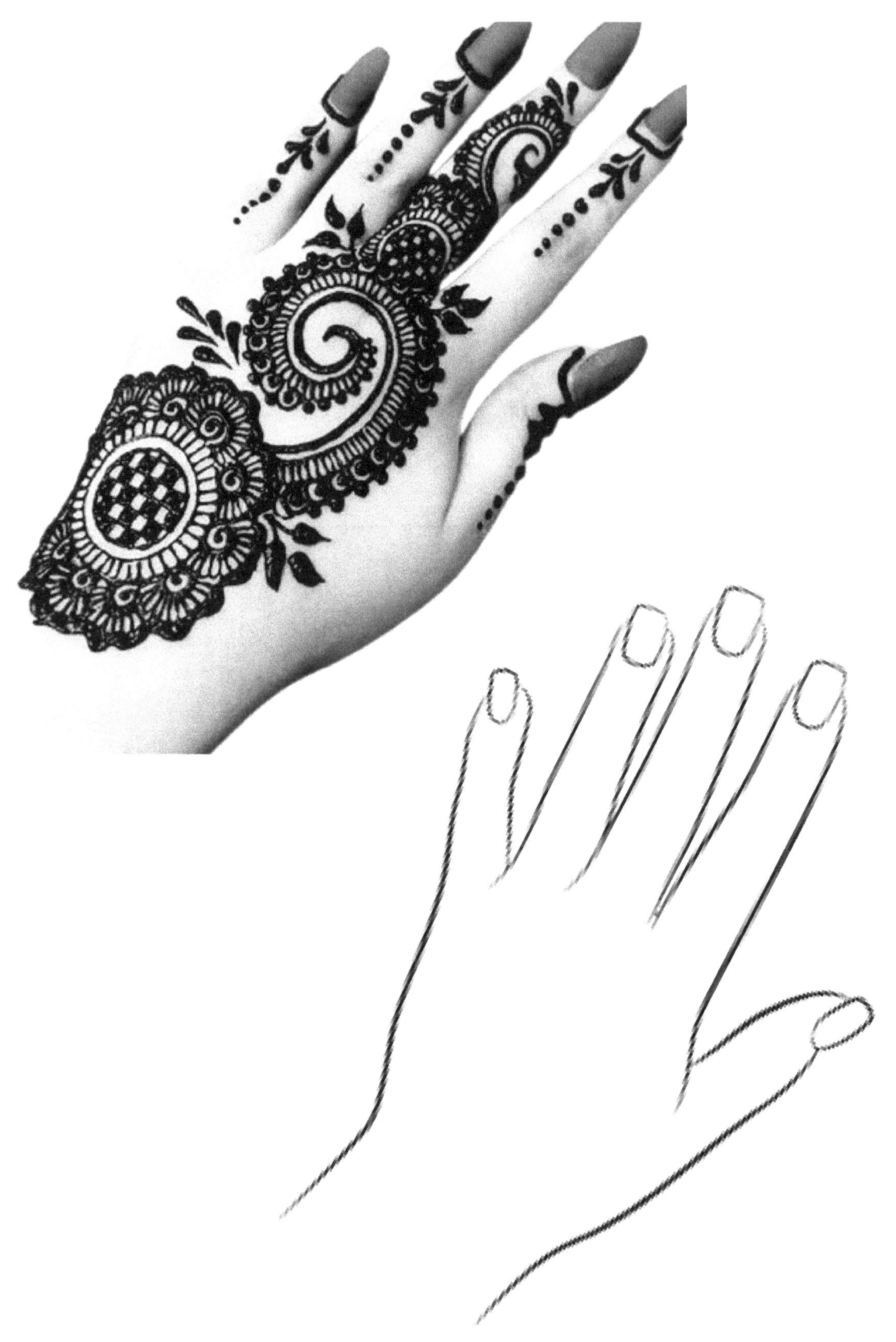

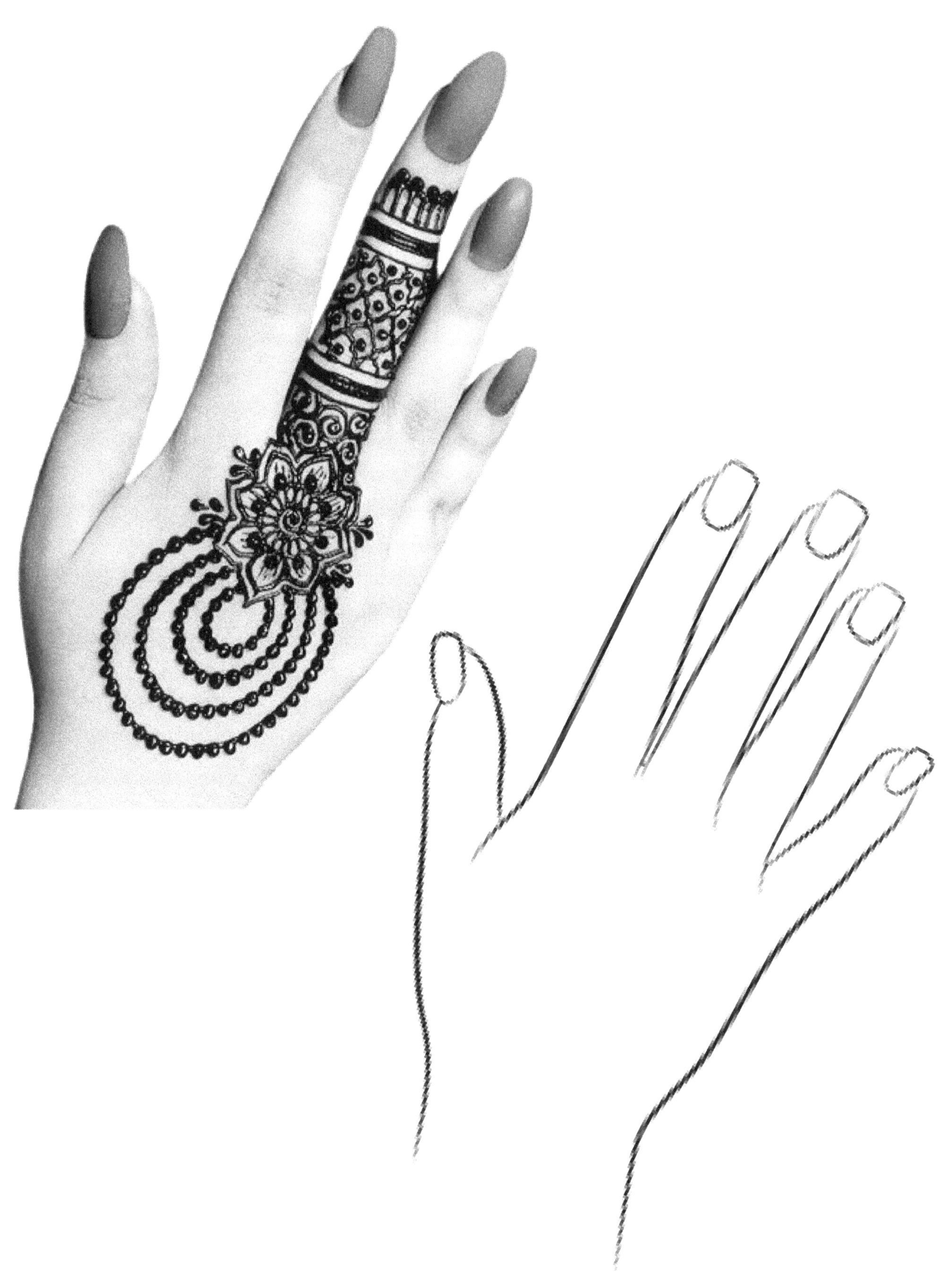

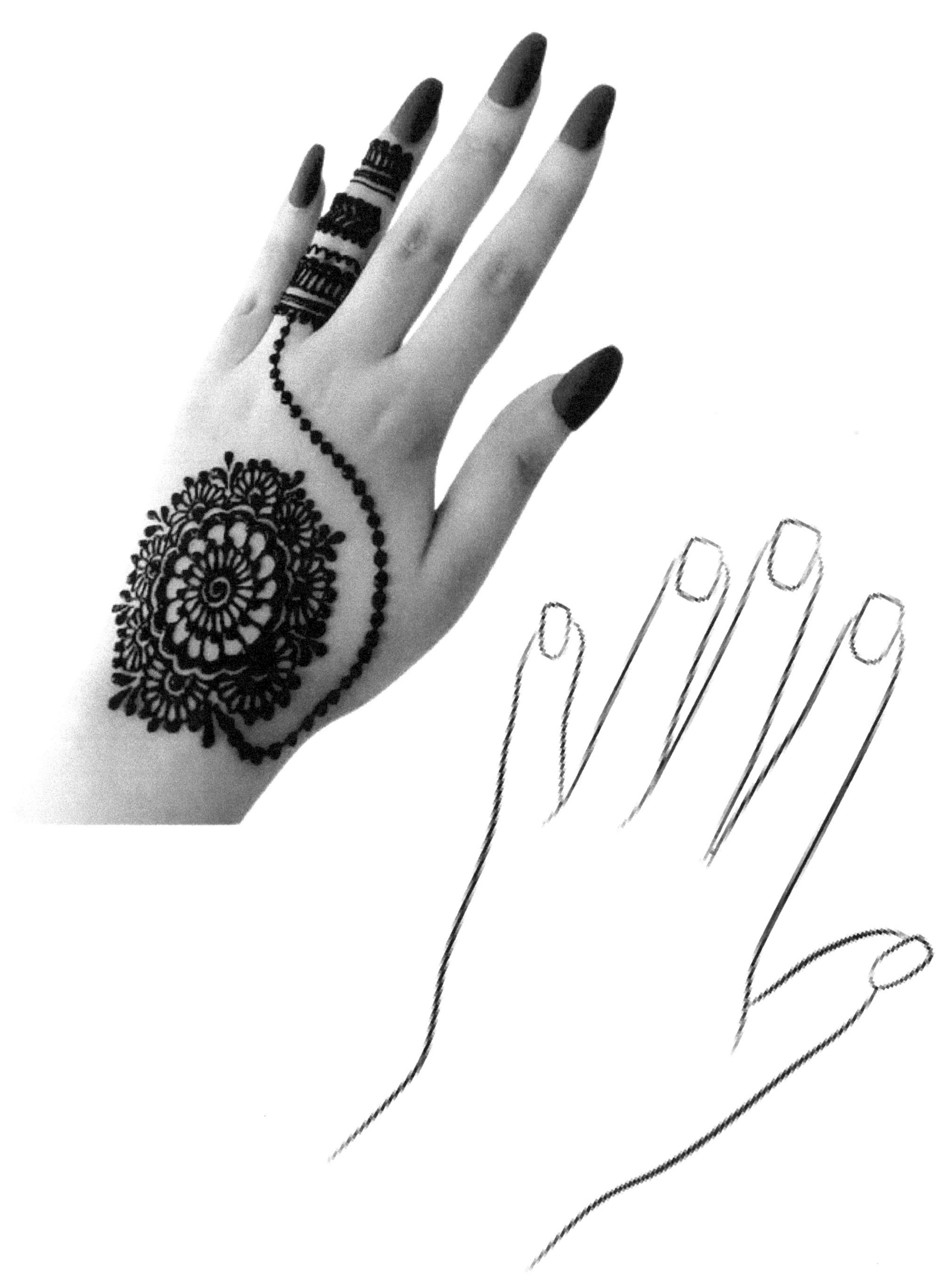

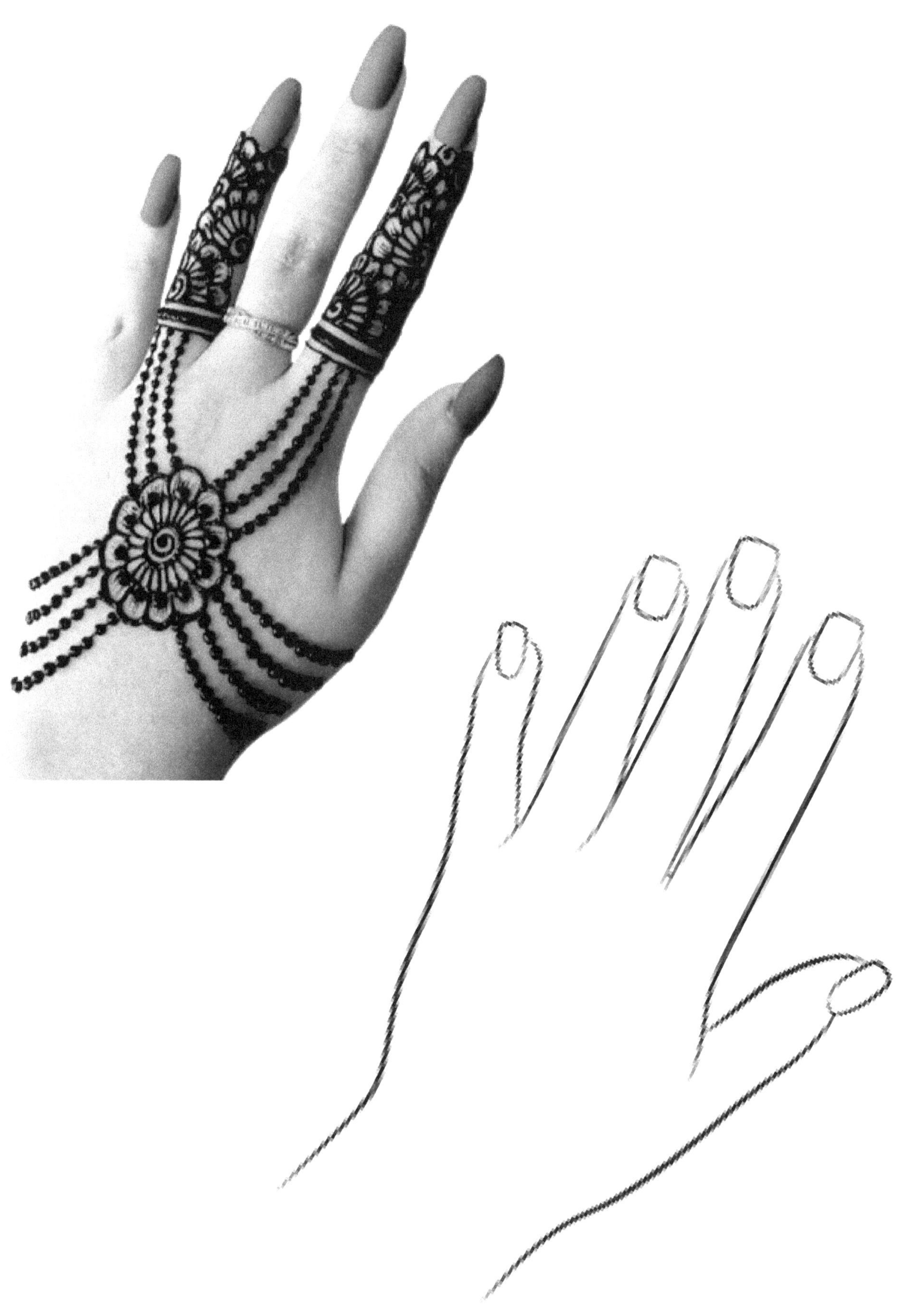

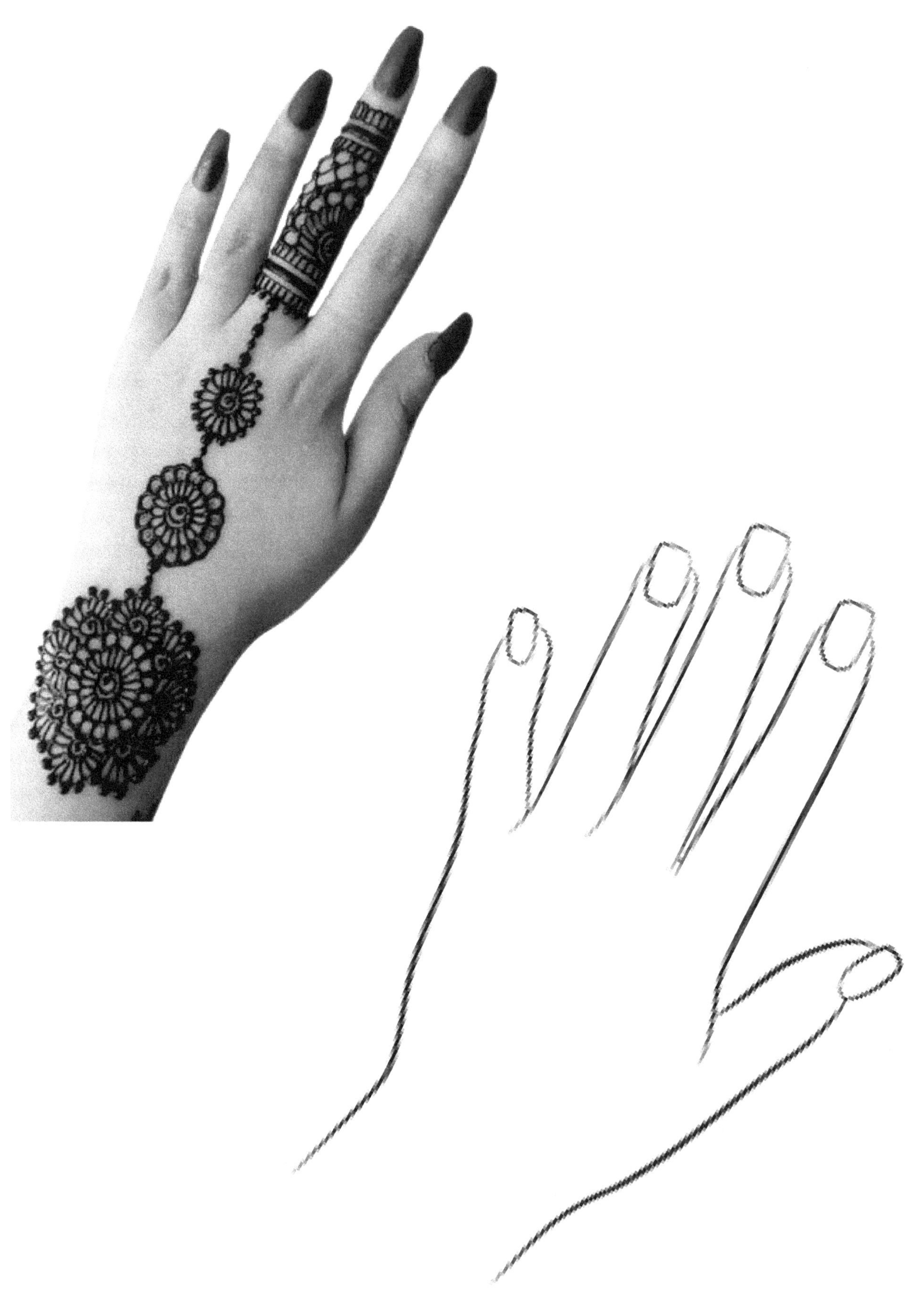

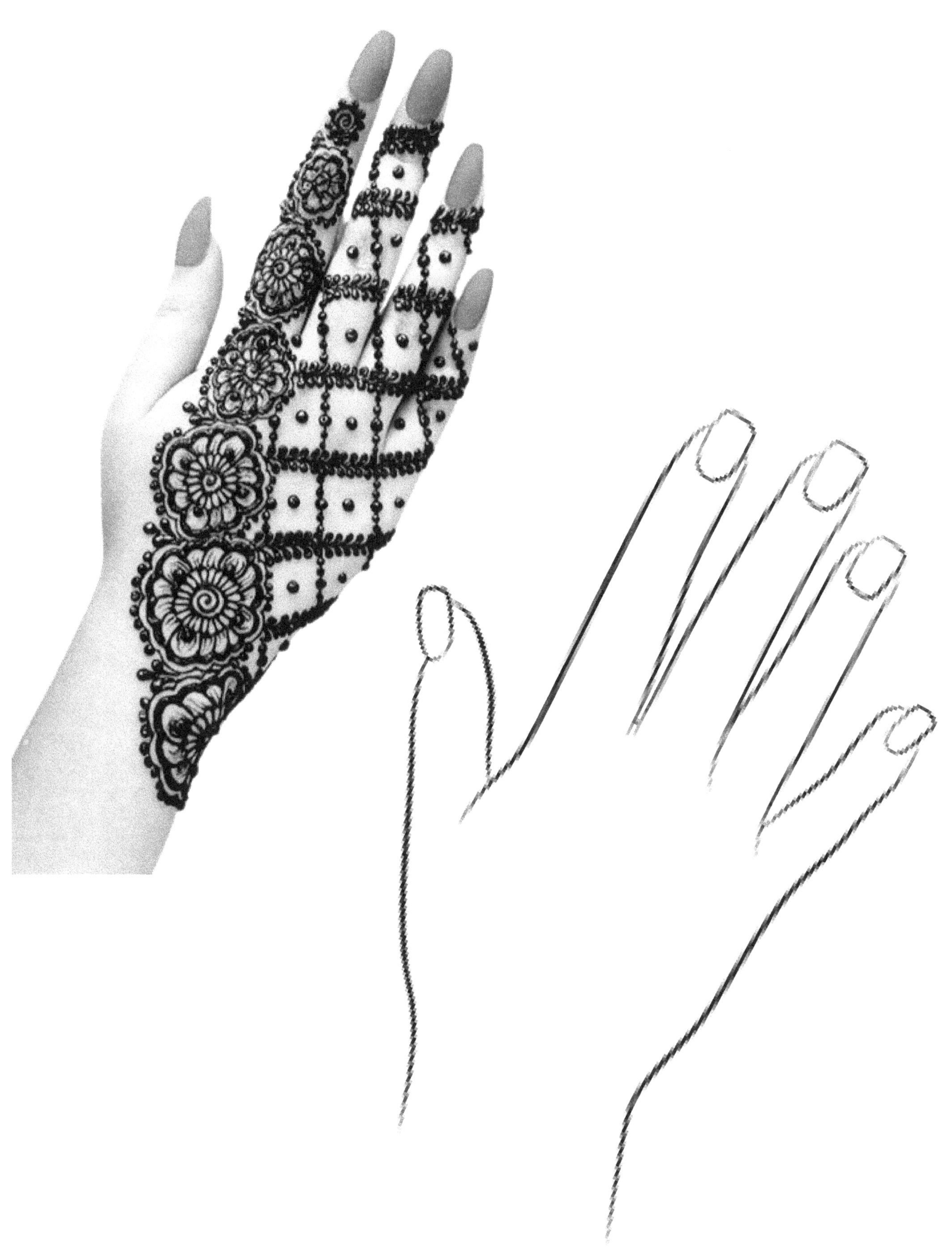

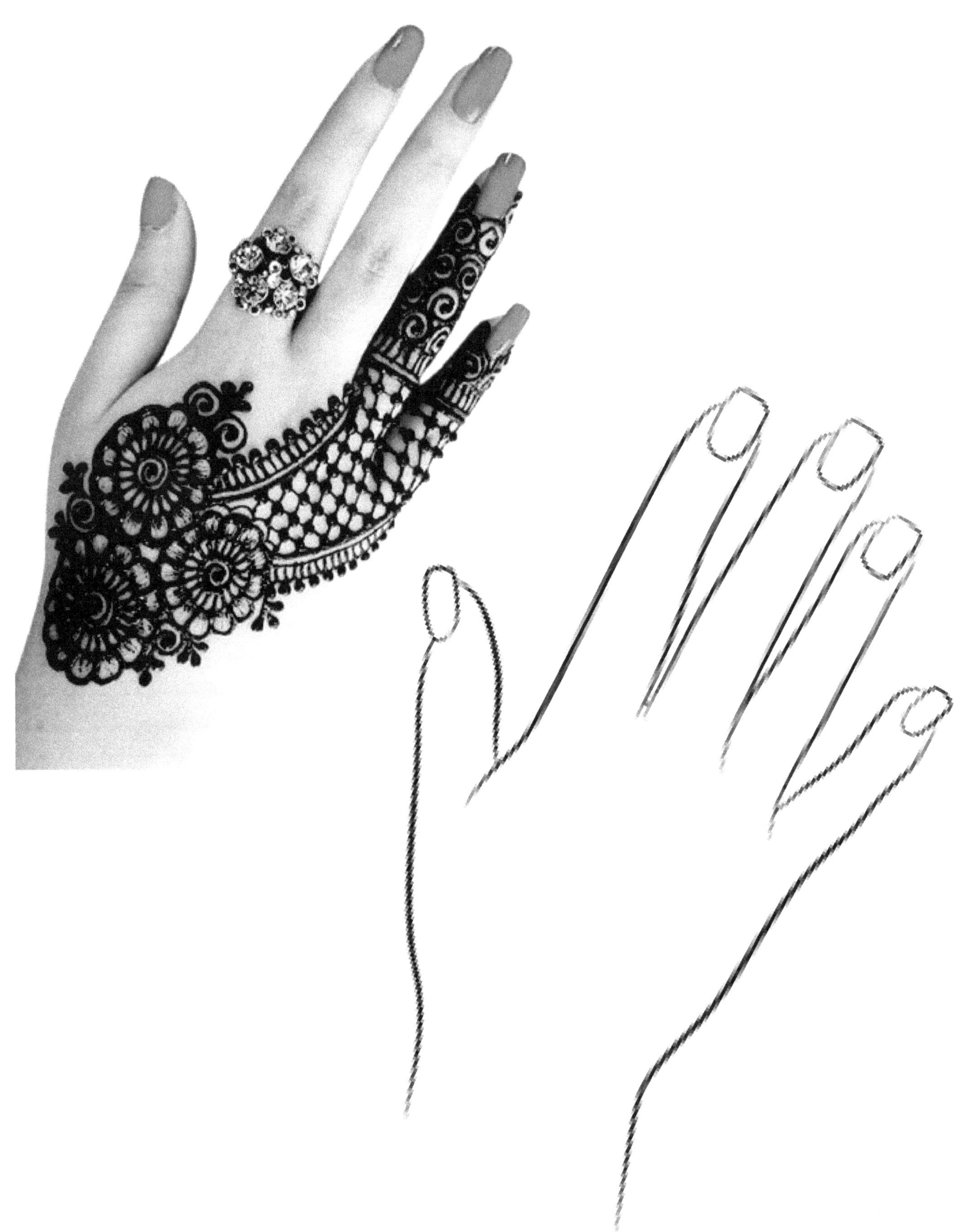

www.ingramcontent.com/pod-product-compliance
Lightning Source LLC
Chambersburg PA
CBHW040217110726
48005CB00019B/3050